CW01432128

Trust-Driven Change: Build Trust. Lead with Clarity. Make It Stick.

Shane A. Wentz, PhD

Copyright © 2025 A Change in Latitude Publishing

All rights reserved

ISBN-979-8-9997172-0-7

To my incredible wife, Susie, and our son, Tommy—
Thank you for your unwavering love, patience, and strength. While I chased meaning, scribbled through late nights, and poured myself into helping others lead through change, you quietly held everything together. This book exists because of your steady presence, your belief in me, and your endless support.

To the many leaders, teammates, and others I've had the privilege to walk alongside—thank you for your trust, your partnership, and your resilience. You've shown me that lasting change doesn't begin with systems or strategies—it begins within. True change is rooted in self-awareness, values, and the courage to grow. Your stories are woven into every chapter of this book

To David, Ty, Brian, Chad, Jerrel and AnnMarie—thank you for being the kind of friends who never disappear when things get hard. You've reminded me that family isn't always about blood, it's about loyalty, laughter, and showing up when it matters most.

To those I served with in uniform, and to the men and women who gave everything in service to our country—your courage and sacrifice will never be forgotten and is an inspiration to me every day.

Finally, to anyone who's ever felt stuck, overwhelmed by change, or unsure of what comes next—this book is for you. You don't need permission to change. You just need the courage to begin. I hope these pages give you the clarity, confidence, and encouragement to take that next step—even when the world refuses to sit still.

Introduction: The Long Game of Change

From a young age, I learned how to adapt to change—not because I wanted to, but because I had to. I grew up in a broken home where stability was rare. With each new relationship my mom entered—and eventually left—the rules of the household shifted. What felt normal one month could feel like a stranger's house the next. I wasn't changing cities, but I was constantly adjusting to new dynamics, new expectations, and a new version of "family" that never seemed to last.

When I joined the military, that cycle continued. Assignments moved us from state to state, base to base. My wife Susie, an amazingly patient and loving partner, learned to spot the look in my eyes when new orders arrived: "Where are we going now?" she'd ask. One week, we were building routines in Washington State; weeks later, I was in Iraq or Kuwait, where trust had to be built quickly and failure wasn't just inconvenient—it was dangerous. In those moments, I learned something critical: trust is the first currency of change. Without it, no amount of authority or skill mattered.

When I left the Army for the corporate world, I thought the turbulence of change might settle down. So did Susie. We were wrong. If anything, the pace was faster. In business, the mission wasn't always clear, structures were less defined, and people often resisted change because they'd seen so many failed initiatives before. I had to relearn how to lead, how to communicate, and how to win people's trust in environments where skepticism was high.

Over the years—in my corporate roles, as a consultant, and as a coach to my son's sports teams, a husband to my wife, a parent, and even a sibling, I've seen the same pattern play out: change isn't just about strategy, systems, or speed. Rather, it rises and falls on trust. That trust isn't confined to boardrooms or factory floors. Parents wrestle with helping their kids navigate the shifting pressures of school, technology, and friendships. Coaches guide athletes through the highs of victory and the lows of defeat as cultural norms, even in sports, change. Teachers, mentors, siblings, and community leaders face the same challenge every day: how do you guide people through uncertainty when the rules seem to shift beneath your feet?

Here's the reality that many of us find so scary: change is accelerating. What used to unfold over years now happens in weeks or even days. This moment—right now—is the least amount of change you will experience in your lifetime. Technology, markets, education, family dynamics, and even our cultural values are evolving at a relentless pace. Those who fail to adapt quickly get left behind, whether they're companies, communities, or individuals.

But here's the hard truth: most people don't love the process of change. They love the promise of change—the better results, the healthier family, the stronger team, the deeper faith. What they don't love is the struggle, the discomfort, and the uncertainty that comes with it. Real change is messy, and it forces us to question old habits, step out of comfort zones, and lean into discomfort. The only way people will willingly walk through that mess is if they trust the leader guiding them—whether that leader is a CEO, a frontline leader, a coach, a parent, or an older sibling.

Maybe you've felt this tension as your organization struggles with new demands, your family wrestles with shifting dynamics, your team is stuck in old habits, or your community is resisting a new direction. If so, you're not alone. I've been there, and I've seen countless others face the same challenge. The secret is simple but not easy: change doesn't stick without trust. It's not about having the best strategy, the loudest voice, or the biggest vision. It's about creating clarity, building ownership, and leading in a way that earns people's belief that change is worth the effort.

The Framework for Lasting Change

That's why I developed a simple framework:

• **Evaluate** – Understand where you are, where you need to go, and why it matters.

• **Execute** – Take disciplined action that drives real results, not just conversations.

• **Sustain** – Embed change into culture through trust, accountability, and continuous progress.

Without this structure, change becomes just another failed initiative, another broken promise, another team, family, or organization stuck in a cycle of "trying something new" without ever succeeding.

Enter Sean: A Leader Thrown into the Fire
This book isn't a lecture or a checklist. It's a story—one grounded in real-life lessons about what it takes to lead meaningful, lasting change. You'll meet Sean, a former Soldier turned turnaround specialist, who's thrown into the chaos of a struggling company. He doesn't get a roadmap, endless resources, or a guaranteed strategy. What he does have is the responsibility to figure it out—just like business leaders, parents, teachers, and coaches everywhere are asked to do every day. As you walk with him through the challenges of pushback, limited resources, tangled systems, and moments of doubt, you'll see the principles of trust-driven change come alive. You'll see how change actually works, not in theory but in practice.

Here's the question I hope this book leaves you with: since you're already standing at the edge of change in your own life—whether in your work, your family, your faith, or your community—are you ready to lead it from within, in a way that builds trust and makes it last?

If so, let's dive in

Chapter 1: The Call

Sean had never been a coffee guy, much to the confusion of his old Army buddies who swore by it. Ten years of early mornings, late-night missions, and lengthy deployments, and he still couldn't stomach the taste. He'd tried it every way imaginable—black, sweetened, drowned in cream, even iced. Nothing worked.

Celsius had become his morning go-to, not just for the flavor, but for the fuel. It powered his 5 a.m. routine: a quick workout, some quiet reflection, and then work. Today was supposed to be more of the same, until the phone rang. The sharp chime sliced through the hum of the ceiling fan and the soft light filtering through the blinds of his home office. On the desk sat his worn-out notebook, a whiteboard filled with scribbled thoughts and sticky notes, and a laptop blinking with unread emails.

The caller ID made him pause. It said "Jake Sr." It had been a few years since they last spoke. Sean's thoughts flicked back to the first time they met, when he was still in the Army, wrestling with the decision to stay in and continue to serve his country or take the leap into civilian life. Jake had been the one who nudged him forward. "You know how to lead," he said. "And out here, leadership is in short supply."

Jake was the big-picture guy. He saw potential in people and opportunity in messes. He had made a career out of buying struggling companies and surrounding himself with people who could bring them back to life—and Sean was one of those people. Sean wasn't a flashy executive or a smooth-talking consultant. He was simply the one who stepped into the noise and helped people find the signal again. His strength wasn't just vision; it was execution. He could take a scattered mess of ideas, plans, and problems and create something steady, simple, and real.

He answered. "Sean here."

"Sean," Jake's voice was brisk and energetic. "I've got something for you, a real opportunity."

Sean leaned back in his chair, already smiling. "A real one? You say that every time."

Jake chuckled. "This one's different. You'll want it."

Sean raised an eyebrow. "That's what worries me."

Jake didn't bite. "It's a manufacturing company with solid products and great market potential, but they're stuck. Leadership turnover, no clear direction, and a team that's starting to check out. Sound familiar?"

Sean exhaled through his nose. "Very familiar," he responded.

"What's the catch?" he asked.

"The usual. Short timeline, tight margins, and skeptical people. But if anyone can steady the ship, it's you."

Sean looked out the window at the calm street below. He had promised his wife, Mary, that he would slow down. Following years of constant movement—deployments, client projects, airports, and all-nighters, they had found a rhythm. They took walks, cooked meals, and Sean's favorite: spent time on the water in their boat. It wasn't retirement; it was reconnection.

Mary had always been the grounding force in his life. A brilliant, driven professional in her own right, she had left a rising corporate career to follow Sean through the chaos of military life. From base housing to deployments and career pivots to cross-country moves, she had shown up with quiet resilience and a spark that never faded.

As if on cue, a text popped up on Sean's phone.

"Jake already called me. I'm in—if you promise I get you back on the boat when this one's done."

Sean laughed. Classic Mary. Permission and a warning, all in one.

He typed back: "Deal. Just don't catch more fish than me this time."

Jake was still on the line. "She's still got your number."

"Always," Sean said. "Send me the details."

"Already on the way. Welcome back to the fight."

When the call ended, Sean stayed in his chair, letting the quiet settle. The world felt loud lately and everyone seemed overwhelmed. Things were moving faster than people could keep up with—technology, expectations, life itself. People weren't just tired; they were stuck.

Yet he knew that change doesn't begin with a plan—it begins with a person. Someone willing to show up, listen, learn, and most importantly lead—not by force, but by trust. That truth wasn't just for boardrooms or shop floors; it was just as real on ballfields, in classrooms, in politics, and within families. Wherever people were being asked to adapt, trust made the difference.

He flipped to a clean page in his notebook and wrote three familiar words:

Evaluate. Execute. Sustain.

This wasn't just another turnaround; it was a chance to prove that even in chaos, progress is possible—and that when you focus on what matters most—people, purpose, and process—you can make change stick.

Over the next few days, Sean dug into research and held phone calls with his new leadership team, piecing together a clearer picture of what he was walking into. The company, Summit Manufacturing, had been a regional leader in specialty industrial components for over two decades. Founded by a brilliant engineer straight out of college, Summit had built a reputation for quality and reliability. But over the past few years, cracks had begun to show. Sales had plateaued and competitors were undercutting them on price. Operational inefficiencies had crept in, driving up costs. Customer complaints were rising, and key employees were leaving. Then there was the elephant in the room: Summit's largest client, a national distributor, had begun shifting orders to a rival. If they lost that account entirely, it would be a financial blow that could put the company into free fall.

The more Sean learned, the clearer it became: Summit wasn't just struggling, it was teetering on the edge of a full-scale crisis. Yet buried in the mess, there were reasons for hope. The company still had skilled people, and it still had customers who wanted it to succeed. It still had a chance to turn things around—but only if they acted fast. Sean exhaled and underlined three words in his notebook:

Stabilize. Simplify. Strengthen.

The words weren't just for Summit. They echoed lessons that had carried him through deployments, cross-country moves, and even evenings helping his son Timmy's baseball team through a rough season. When things feel uncertain—whether you're running a company, leading a family, or coaching a team, the first step is the same: steady the ground beneath you, simplify what matters most, and then build the strength to move forward.

Chapter 2: Sean's Journey

A few days later, Sean was on a plane heading to the company's headquarters in Chicago. He closed his notebook and leaned back in his seat, staring at the ceiling of the plane. The spark of excitement from Jake's call was tempered by the enormity of the task ahead. He knew from experience that the first days in any new role were crucial, especially when stepping into a struggling organization that needed to be turned around quickly. The decisions made—or not made—and actions taken during those early moments would set the tone for everything that followed.

Sean had spent almost a decade walking into struggling organizations, tasked with quickly turning things around. Some of those companies had been on the verge of collapse—bleeding cash, riddled with inefficiencies, crippled by broken leadership. Others simply lacked direction, drifting without a clear strategy or the discipline to execute one.

At its core, Sean knew that real leadership was about guiding meaningful change in habits, systems, relationships, and mindsets that reshape how people work and connect. It wasn't about sweeping overhauls, but rather intentional steps that added up over time. He pulled out his notebook, flipping to an empty page. At the top, he wrote one word: **Listen**

That would be his top priority early on—not charging in with pre-packaged solutions or handing down mandates from the executive suite. Listening. Because if there was one thing Sean had learned over the years, it was that people weren't resistant to change itself but were resistant to being changed by someone who hadn't earned their trust. Change needed to be something Sean did with the employees of the company—not to them.

Listening wasn't passive. It was an act of leadership, and it helped build trust. In *The Speed of Trust*, Stephen M.R. Covey wrote, "Trust is the one thing that changes everything." When employees trust their leaders, engagement rises, innovation flourishes, and organizations adapt more effectively. Building that trust required more than words—it demanded consistent, intentional actions that showed respect for their experiences and insights.

As he watched the city lights flicker below, Sean reflected on his own journey of change that had started at an early age.

The Making of a Leader

Sean had grown up in Ohio, early on moving frequently as a military brat, then settling down in Lancaster, a small town just south of Columbus. His mother had been married and divorced several times, always chasing a better future that never quite materialized. For Sean and his brother, John, stability was a rare luxury. They learned early on how to adapt, how to blend into new schools, how to survive in homes where love often felt conditional.

With their mother rarely around, Sean took on the role of both older brother and borderline parent. It forced him to mature far sooner than any child should have—but it also began shaping his values.

At one point, his mother moved in with a new boyfriend, leaving Sean and his brother with his stepdad—a man who was as erratic as he was unpredictable. He wasn't just a poor role model; he was actively destructive. He abused drugs, was quick to anger, and had little patience for a kid he often reminded, "was not his."

For Sean, home was a place to endure, not embrace. He learned to stay quiet, to avoid confrontation, and often to blend into the background. But deep down, even as a child, he knew he wanted something different.

He didn't want to repeat the cycle of broken relationships, empty promises, and wasted potential. He didn't want to be another person who blamed their circumstances for their failures. He wanted to build a life he could be proud of.

Later in life, he would come to embrace the concept of $\mathbf{E} + \mathbf{R} = \mathbf{O}$ — Event plus Response equals Outcome. In other words, while you may not control the events around you, your response most definitely shapes the outcome.

Sports as an Escape

By high school, sports had become more than just an extracurricular activity; they were his sanctuary. The football field and baseball diamond weren't just places to compete—they were places where effort equaled reward, where discipline created opportunities, and where success was earned, not given.

His teammates became more than just friends; they were family. Far more involved in his life than his mother, they—along with his brother, coaches, his new stepdad Mike, and a few teachers—had the most influence on Sean at an early age.

Chad was his catcher when he pitched for the high school baseball team. Always quick to pick Sean up, not just when he was having a bad game, but when things at home got dark. One night, after a particularly bad fight with his mom, Chad and his mother let Sean stay over. His mom tried to come get him, but Chad's mom threatened to call the police if she didn't leave.

Ty and Brian were two of Sean's best friends, also on the baseball team. The three of them were inseparable, and their bond on and off the field earned them the nickname "The Bad Boys"—likely due to their impressive party résumé as much as their ballgame bravado.

Then there was Jerrel. They'd grown close on the football team, though things got a bit complicated when Sean started dating Jerrel's sister. Still, their friendship held strong, and Sean spent so much time at their house that Jerrel's parents used to joke that if the doorbell rang around dinnertime, it was probably Sean.

He wasn't a natural athlete, but he was relentless. His hatred of losing was only surpassed by his commitment to getting better—and his coaches noticed.

"You're not the fastest," his football coach, Buck, once told him. "You're not the biggest either. But you're the guy who shows up early, stays late, and refuses to quit. That's why people follow you."

Sean often reflected on that. Leadership wasn't about talent or title, it was about effort, consistency, and lifting others up.

In one defining moment, Sean learned the power of focus under pressure. It was the state baseball tournament. Bases loaded. Two outs. Two strikes. The stadium noise faded as he locked in.

From the third base line, his coach shouted,
"Don't try to hit a home run, just make contact."

Sean exhaled, stepped back into the box, and trusted his swing. The next pitch came—

Crack!

The ball sailed high over the fence for a home run, and the right fielder didn't even move as the crowd erupted. Sean only found out later that the ball had smashed the window of his coach's parents' car. It wasn't just a walk-off—it was a reminder: under pressure, trust your preparation and don't overcomplicate things. That lesson would serve him well for the rest of his life.

Lessons from the Military

Perhaps nothing shaped Sean's approach to leadership more than his time in the Army. He enlisted straight out of college, looking to make a difference and serve his country. Over the course of a decade, he deployed multiple times and held various leadership roles.

The military had a way of stripping away the unnecessary. It taught him what truly mattered in leadership:
  – Action matters more than plans.
  – Plans are great, but adaptability is essential.
  – Trust is built through action, not words.
  – No one succeeds alone.

It was in the Army that Sean first developed what would become his core leadership framework:

Evaluate. Execute. Sustain.

At first, Sean didn't think of himself as a fixer. He was just a Soldier doing the job—following orders, completing missions, moving from one assignment to the next. But a pattern began to emerge. He kept being assigned to underperforming units. Places where discipline had slipped. Where morale was low. Where communication was broken. Places others wanted to avoid.

Over time, senior leaders started pulling him aside with quiet, unofficial requests:

"Keep an eye on that team."

"See if you can steady the ship."

He didn't have a formal title or special authority. What he did have was presence. He showed up consistently. He asked good questions and didn't pretend to have all the answers. When it was time to lead, people followed—not because they had to, but because they trusted him.

That's when it clicked. Leadership wasn't about position; it was about influence. Real influence—the kind you earn by listening first and built on trust and authenticity, not ego.

Early in his military career, Sean had embraced a definition of leadership that stuck with him: *"Leadership is the ability to influence others to accomplish the mission by providing purpose, direction, and motivation."*

That definition became more than a motto—it became the lens through which he saw every leadership challenge ahead.

A Defining Moment

One deployment in particular drove the lesson home. Sean had been assigned to a unit with a reputation for dysfunction. They were responsible for convoy security, but their preparation was sloppy.

Vehicles weren't properly checked, radios didn't work, and communication was chaotic.

One night, before a mission, Sean watched Soldiers rushing through their checks. He stopped them cold.

"We're not rolling out like this."

There were groans and eye rolls because nobody wanted a delay. But Sean stood his ground as he walked the team through every detail—ensuring vehicles, weapons, and comms systems were squared away.

That night, their convoy hit an IED, an improvised explosive device. Because of the extra preparation, they responded with calm and coordination. The radios worked, and everyone knew the plan, resulting in no injuries. Sean never forgot the lesson of that deployment: leadership wasn't about speed; it was about readiness—and the best fix was the one that would last.

From Military to Mission

As he transitioned out of uniform, Sean carried that mindset into his civilian career. He realized that every broken process, every disengaged team, and every burned-out leader could be addressed through one framework:

Evaluate – Before acting, seek to understand. Observe the work. Talk to the people closest to the problem. Listen with humility.

Execute – Take action with precision and speed. Include the people doing the work in designing the fix. Focus on simple solutions with clear ownership.

Sustain – Build systems and habits that last. Empower teams. Ensure the change outlives the leader who started it.

And perhaps most importantly—don't impose change on people. Create the conditions for change to be done with them, not to them.

That simple framework became Sean's compass, whether he was leading a project, coaching a team, trying to understand why Mary was upset with him, or stepping into a company on the brink.

The Road Ahead

As the plane began its descent, Sean flipped to a clean page in his notebook and wrote down one final reminder:

People don't resist change, they resist uncertainty.

Give them clarity and direction as well as a reason to believe. And always answer the why behind the change—even if the answer is hard to hear.

He closed his notebook, stretched his arms, and looked out the window as the lights of Chicago came into view. One last sip of wine, and after a good night's sleep, it would be time to go to work.

Chapter 3: Bathroom-Based Business Analysis

The next morning, as Sean walked into the company's headquarters for the first time, he took in the details that told a story about the status of the organization. Chipped paint on the walls, scattered desks that screamed disorganization, and the muted energy of employees going through the motions—all signs of a company that had been in survival mode for far too long. He felt a sense of empathy. These employees weren't just part of a broken system; they had been trapped in it.

Sean knew that the real story of an organization wasn't always found in its policies or performance metrics; it was in the places people overlooked.

He recalled a lesson from one of his earliest mentors, James, a gruff but insightful operations leader who initially did not like Sean. They had worked together at one of the turnarounds Sean was leading, and James thought Sean was too young and inexperienced to be in the position he was in.

While Scan didn't exactly disagree, he was often at odds with James. So, he went to his assistant, found out James's travel schedule, and showed up at the hotel bar one night when James was sitting alone having dinner. They talked, ate, and drank for over four hours, and from that point on they worked great together.

During a manufacturing site visit together, James suddenly stopped Sean outside the employee restroom.

"Sean," James said, his tone serious, "do you know what one of the most telling places in any organization is?"

Caught off guard, Sean hesitated. "The production line? The breakroom?"

James shook his head. "The bathroom."

James leaned against the doorway, arms crossed, and continued:

"Think about it. The bathroom is where employees go when no one's watching. It's not where customers walk through, and it's not where leadership holds meetings. It's the one place in a company that isn't designed for appearances. Because of that, it's one of the best indicators of how much, or how little, a company values its people."

Sean nodded slowly, his mind replaying memories of past workplaces. The pristine office spaces with gleaming conference rooms, but bathrooms that smelled and looked like neglect. The companies that preached about employee well-being but had stalls with broken locks, empty soap dispensers, and floors that hadn't seen a mop in weeks. He had always brushed it off—just another facility issue, nothing worth thinking about. But now, James had him seeing it in an entirely new light.

"When leadership walks through the building, they see what they want to see," James continued. "They see the production floor when

16

it's been prepped for a tour. They see reports and dashboards. But they don't see the places that tell the truth."

Sean folded his arms, intrigued. "And the bathroom tells the truth?"

James smirked. "Go check for yourself. You'll learn more in sixty seconds in there than in an hour-long meeting."

Sean wasn't one to take things at face value. So, later that day, between meetings, he took James up on his challenge. He walked into the employee restroom near the production floor—not the one by the executive offices where the site leader had encouraged him to go.

The first thing he noticed was the smell: stale air mixed with industrial cleaners that clearly hadn't been used recently. A toilet seat was cracked, held together with tape. The soap dispensers were nearly empty, and one had a handwritten note stuck to it: *"Out of Order. Again."* The paper towel dispenser was broken, leaving employees to shake their hands dry or wipe them on their pants. Sean exhaled slowly; James was right.

He imagined a worker on their break, stepping away for a moment of personal time, only to be met with this. What did it say about the company? About leadership? But then another thought hit him. What did it say about the employees?

A bathroom in this state didn't just reflect how leadership viewed its workers, it reflected how workers viewed themselves and their environment. If no one bothered to clean up after themselves, if employees saw overflowing trash cans and empty soap dispensers and simply shrugged, what else were they willing to ignore? If they didn't take pride in keeping the space they used every day in decent condition, how much pride did they take in their work?

He had seen it before in other companies. The ones where employees tossed their trash on the floor instead of using a can, where tools were left scattered instead of returned to their places, where people only did the bare minimum because no one expected more. A bathroom in disrepair wasn't just a sign of bad management—it was a sign of a culture that had given up.

Later, as he and James walked around the production floor together, Sean turned to him. "You were right. That bathroom told me everything I needed to know."

James smiled. "And?"

Sean shook his head. "The company doesn't care about the employees, and the employees don't care about the company."

James nodded. "That's how it goes. A company that doesn't value its people will eventually have people who don't value their work. It always starts small: dirty bathrooms, messy breakrooms, tools left out. But it spreads, and people stop seeing themselves as part of something bigger. They stop taking ownership."

Sean thought back to some of the companies he had worked with. The ones where employees wiped down their stations at the end of every shift, where shared spaces were kept in order without being told, where even the bathrooms were clean—not because management enforced it, but because the people who worked there had pride in their environment. That pride bled into everything else they did.

"So, what's the fix?" Sean asked.

James exhaled. "It's not just about hiring more janitors, if that's what you're thinking."

Sean chuckled. "No, I got that much."

James nodded. "It's about resetting expectations. Leaders must show, through their actions and words, that they care—fix the bathrooms, stock the soap, replace what's broken. But then, employees need to step up too. They need to see that it's their space, their company, their work. If they don't take pride in the little things, they won't take pride in the big ones either."

Sean let that sit for a moment. He had always known that culture wasn't dictated by mission statements or motivational posters, but he had never considered how much it could be revealed by something as simple as a bathroom. It wasn't just true in business; pride in the small things showed up everywhere—in a kid's sports team keeping their dugout clean, in families who respected shared spaces at home, in communities where neighbors picked up trash that wasn't theirs. Big change rarely started with grand gestures; it began with how people handled the little things.

Years later, that lesson had become second nature to Sean. During a site visit with his boss, Shawn (great first name, he always said), a CEO he deeply respected, Sean had walked straight to the restroom upon arrival.

When he emerged, his face betrayed nothing. But as he approached Shawn, the CEO looked at him with furrowed brows. "Are you okay?" he asked, genuine concern in his voice.

Sean was momentarily confused. "Yeah, why?"

Shawn gestured toward the restroom. "It's just… every time we visit a site, you head straight to the bathroom. I was starting to think you had some kind of problem."

Sean burst out laughing. "No, boss. I check the bathroom because it's the fastest way to figure out what's really going on here."

Shawn raised an eyebrow, skeptical. "What could a bathroom possibly tell you about a business?"

Sean relayed James's wisdom. "If the bathroom is dirty, broken, or neglected, it's a sign that leadership isn't paying attention to the basics. If they're not taking care of their employees, they're probably not taking care of the business either."

Shawn thought for a moment. "So, what did you learn this time?"

Sean smiled. "Let's just say that bathroom needs more attention than our financial statements. No soap, two out of three stalls out of order, and a broken paper towel holder replaced by a roll stacked on the counter. If that's how they treat something as basic as a restroom, imagine how they treat their people."

From that day on, the running joke between them was Sean's "bathroom test." Every time they traveled together, Shawn would quip, "Ready for your first inspection?" But behind the humor, he had come to respect the method. Over time, he noticed the pattern: facilities with clean, well-maintained restrooms had higher morale and better performance. Those with neglected restrooms had deeper issues.

Years later, when Sean left that company for a new leadership role, Shawn sent him a farewell email with a single line: *May your next restroom inspections be as insightful as ever.*

Now, standing in the hallway of his new company, Sean glanced toward the employee's restroom. If the state of the building was any indication, he already had an idea of what he'd find. But habits were habits, and this one had never steered him wrong.

As he pushed open the door, the first thing he noticed was the smell—not offensive, but stale, like cleaning had been rushed or skipped. A fluorescent light flickered, casting a dim glow over cracked tiles. A slow, rhythmic drip echoed from a faucet wrapped in a rag, a clear DIY fix. Two of three stalls were occupied; the third had an "Out of Order" sign with curled edges, as if it had been there for months. No soap in the dispensers. A roll of paper towels stacked on the counter. The trash bin overflowed.

Sean took it all in. Every detail confirmed what he suspected: this company wasn't just struggling operationally; it had lost its sense of pride.

The door swung open behind him. A middle-aged employee in a worn uniform stepped inside, hesitating when he saw Sean. His eyes flicked to the overflowing trash, the broken stall, the grimy sink.

Sean turned to him. "How long has it been like this?"

The man sighed, moving to the sink to wash his hands. "Months. Complained a few times, but…" He trailed off, drying his hands on his jeans. "Guess we all just stopped expecting anything to change."

Sean absorbed that. It wasn't the broken stall or the lack of soap that mattered most—it was the resignation in the man's voice. That quiet acceptance that things were the way they were and wouldn't get better.

This was more than a failing organization; this was a place where hope had eroded. Sean exhaled slowly, nodding. "That's about to change."

The employee gave him a skeptical glance but said nothing. Sean didn't expect to win anyone over in a bathroom visit, but he had everything he needed to know. Walking out, he made an entry in his notebook:

Culture isn't what you say, it's what you tolerate. And right now, they are tolerating mediocrity. That is about to end.

Sean had learned long ago that culture doesn't come from mission statements or posters on the wall; it comes from leadership. From what leaders reward, what they ignore, and what they're willing to walk past without saying a word. The fastest way to kill pride in a workplace is to allow subpar standards to go unchecked.

He knew that employees took their cues from the top. If leaders accepted disrepair, disorder, or indifference, then those behaviors would spread. Not because people didn't care, but because they assumed no one else did. And if no one else cared, why should they?

That's why Sean paid attention to the details. Not because bathrooms were a metric of success, but because they were a mirror of the culture. And culture—whether strong or broken—reflects leadership. Leaders shape it every day, in every interaction, with every decision. Sean wasn't just here to improve operations or drive results; he was here to rebuild pride.

In addition, he wanted to raise the standard and ensure the message was clear: we don't tolerate mediocrity, and we don't overlook the little things—because the little things are where culture lives.

Chapter 4: Setting the Table

As Sean walked into the conference room, he carried two large boxes of bagels and several carafes of coffee. The aroma of fresh coffee and warm pastries filled the air as the leadership team began trickling in. A few hesitant glances were exchanged; no one was used to this kind of gesture.

David, the company's seasoned Chief Operating Officer, raised an eyebrow. "What's the occasion?"

Sean set the food on the table and smiled. "No occasion," he said. "I just figured we could all use some fuel for what's ahead. And don't worry," he added, glancing at Marcus, the CFO, "this came out of my pocket, not the company's."

Marcus smiled, grabbed a bagel, and nodded. "Well, you're already off to a better start than the last guy."

Sean chuckled but let the comment pass. As the team settled in, he made mental notes about where people chose to sit. Some clustered toward the middle of the table, engaged and ready to contribute, while others hovered near the edges, arms crossed, observing rather than participating.

At the far end, Ray, Director of Operations, sat stiffly, his expression skeptical. Sean recognized the look. It wasn't defiance; it was weariness. Ray had likely seen too many leaders come in with grand promises only to disappear when the real work started. Winning him over wouldn't happen in a single meeting, but Sean was in no rush.

Nelson Mandela and the Circle of Leadership

"Thanks for making time this morning," Sean began. "Before we dive in, I want to share a story that's helped shape the way I think about leadership."

He leaned forward slightly, making eye contact with each leader in the room. "Many of you have probably heard of Nelson Mandela, but what you might not know is that Mandela credited much of his leadership philosophy to his father, a tribal leader in South Africa. Mandela once said that when his father gathered the elders, they always sat in a circle—no head of the table, no seat of power. His father believed that leadership wasn't about taking control through talking or where you sat, but about listening first.

"I want to spend time today listening to all of you. Hearing what has worked and what hasn't worked."

A beat of silence followed before Karen, the Facilities Manager, spoke up. "So, no PowerPoint today?"

Sean grinned. "No PowerPoint," he confirmed. "Today is about us. I want to hear your thoughts, your concerns, and your ideas."

Identifying the Roadblocks

Sean walked to the whiteboard and wrote a simple question:

What's holding us back?

David spoke first. "We're stuck in old habits. People do things the way they always have, even if it's inefficient."

Karen nodded. "We don't communicate well between departments. Everyone's focused on their own piece of the puzzle and not the bigger picture."

Marcus added, "We've had good ideas before, but they never go anywhere. We talk about change, but we don't follow through."

Sean nodded. "Fair points. So, how do we get unstuck?"

Marcus hesitated. "Start smaller. Focus on a few quick wins before we try to fix everything at once."

Sean jotted it down on the whiteboard.

Smart, Practical, actionable steps that build momentum.

Ray exhaled sharply. "And when this turns into just another flavor-of-the-month initiative?"

Sean turned to him. "It won't. But that's not just up to me; it's up to all of us. If we do this right, this won't be an initiative; it will become how we operate."

Introducing the Framework

Sean wrote three bold words on the board:

Evaluate. Execute. Sustain.

"This," he said, turning back to them, "is our framework for success. Every decision, every action, every step forward will come back to these three words."

David spoke up. "So instead of talking about our financial reports, client dissatisfaction, and high turnover, we're talking about three words?"

Sean leaned against the table, unfazed. "Yes. And here's why."

He tapped the first word: **Evaluate.** "We must be brutally honest about where we stand. No sugarcoating, no blame—just clarity. If we can't face reality, we can't fix it."

Next, he tapped **Execute.** "Once we know the right moves, we act. Not just talk—execute with discipline and focus. Ideas don't change outcomes—action does."

Finally, he underlined **Sustain.** "Most transformations fail because they're short-term fixes. If we don't build habits that make change stick—habits that outlast any one leader or initiative—then we're wasting our time."

Ray leaned forward, arms still crossed, eyes narrowing slightly. "And if it doesn't work?"

His tone wasn't sarcastic—but it wasn't hopeful either. It was the voice of someone who had seen a dozen initiatives come and go, each one launched with fanfare and abandoned the moment it got hard.

Sean met his eyes without hesitation. "Then we adjust and try again. But we don't stop."

Ray raised an eyebrow. "That easy, huh?"

Sean smiled faintly. "I didn't say it would be easy. I said we don't stop."

He paused, letting the weight of his response settle in the room.

"We're not aiming for perfection out of the gate. We're going to apply scientific thinking—just like the best organizations in the world do. We'll test ideas, gather feedback, and learn as we go. If something doesn't work, that's not failure—it's feedback. It's a chance to learn, to adapt, and to grow."

Ray crossed his arms tighter. "Yeah, well, around here failure usually comes with finger-pointing and paperwork."

Sean nodded. "That's part of what must change. If people are afraid to fail, they'll never take smart risks. And if we can't take smart risks, we'll never move forward. Failure, when owned and examined, is just feedback. It tells us what to try next."

He paused, then added, "But let me be clear—I'm not here to run experiments that go nowhere. I'm here to build something that works and that lasts. The only way we do that is together—by staying in motion, even when it's uncomfortable."

He looked around the room, making eye contact with each leader.

"We are not here to chase perfection. We're here to pursue progress. The only real failure is doing nothing—or giving up when things get hard. What matters is that we stay in motion, stay transparent, and stay aligned and committed. That's how we'll turn this place around."

Ray didn't say anything else, but Sean could see something shift in his expression—not agreement, necessarily, but a spark of respect. The kind that only comes when someone realizes they're not dealing with another empty suit, but a leader willing to step into the mess and figure it out—with them.

A beat of silence followed. Then Karen exhaled and nodded. "Alright. Let's see where this goes."

Marcus smirked. "Well, we're in it now."

Ray simply leaned back. Sean knew that when the rest of the team started moving forward, Ray would either have to come along, or a necessary conversation would be had.

Chapter 5: Leading Change

The hum of machinery, the rhythmic clang of metal pressing into shape, and the occasional hiss of steam filled the air as Sean stepped onto the factory floor for the first time.

Sean took a deep breath, absorbing the scent of oil, metal, and hot plastic. This was the heartbeat of the operation. The facility housed nearly half of the company's workforce and was responsible for manufacturing high-performance metal components that powered the company's reputation in the market. If real change was going to take hold, it wouldn't start in a conference room or from behind a dashboard—it would start here.

Sean had always believed that leadership didn't live in corner offices or conference rooms. It lived on the floor, in the breakrooms, and out by the shipping dock—anywhere real work was happening, and people were showing up. That's where trust was built—or broken—and where culture wasn't something talked about in all-hands meetings, but something you could feel. Leadership was presence, not position, and influence, not title. He'd seen too many organizations try to drive change from a distance—executives issuing directives from boardrooms, buried in dashboards, removed from the very people expected to implement the change. They talked about change but never left their comfort zone to witness the day-to-day realities of those they led. That type of leadership, in Sean's experience, failed every time.

Because you can't change what you don't understand, and you can't understand what you don't see for yourself. In Sean's mind, leadership wasn't about proximity to power; it was about proximity to people. He didn't believe in managing from a spreadsheet or leading by email. Real leadership required presence, and that meant walking the floor, asking questions, noticing the details others overlooked. It meant showing up—not to inspect, but to connect.

He was a firm believer in going to the *gemba*—the place where the real work happens. Not to inspect, but to understand; to listen and to learn. Because the truth is, the people doing the work every day are the real subject-matter experts. They know what's broken, what gets in the way, and where the opportunities lie; unfortunately, far too often no one ever asks them or listens to their ideas.

As Sean walked through the rows of equipment and workstations, he nodded to the operators, maintenance techs, and team leaders. Some returned the gesture, while others looked surprised to see a CEO walking on the floor without a clipboard or a trail of executives in tow. Sean smiled to himself; that was exactly the reaction he wanted.

Change wouldn't come from talking about culture; it would come from building one—on the floor, side by side with his team, one conversation at a time. His leadership team had asked if he wanted them to join him while he walked around where the work was happening, and he politely explained that just this one time, he thought it better he walk by himself.

Sean took his time walking around the production floor and couldn't help but see the inefficiencies. There were stations waiting on parts that were stuck upstream; machines idling while operators tried to find something; and pallets of raw materials cluttering the aisles, forcing workers to maneuver around them. Several presses also had handwritten notes taped to the sides: *"Out of order."*

The First Opportunity

Workers gave him cautious nods, their eyes flicking between him and their tasks. Some machines ran steadily, but others sat idle, half-finished parts stacked next to them. Then he heard it: a loud metallic clank followed by silence. Sean turned toward one of the larger press machines, where a small team stood around a control panel. One operator adjusted something, stepped back... and waited. A minute passed, another adjustment, and another pause.

Sean saw Bill, the supervisor. "Morning."

Sean returned it. "Morning, Bill. How's it going?"

Bill glanced at the press, then back at him. "Same as yesterday, same as last year."

Sean caught the hint of something in his tone—not defiance, but a quiet resignation. This wasn't just a shop-floor problem; it was a trust problem.

Sean nodded toward the machine. "What's going on here?"

One of the operators, still focused on the screen, muttered, "Die change. We're trying to get the alignment right."

Bill exhaled sharply. "Every damn time."

Sean raised an eyebrow. "How long does this usually take?"

Bill scratched his chin. "It depends; could be twenty minutes, could be an hour. The press won't run if it's not right."

Sean smiled. "Well, let's see if we can change that."

Bill shook his head. "I'll believe it when I see it."

"How often do you change dies?" Sean asked.

Bill frowned. "At least six times a shift."

Sean did some quick math in his head. If each changeover took 30 to 60 minutes, they were losing up to six hours of production time per shift—just standing around, tweaking setups.

Bill seemed to read his mind. "Yeah, it's a pain in the ass."

"So, what's the process for setting up dies?" Sean asked.

The operator, clearly trying to focus, just shook his head. "Uh... well, we just adjust until it's right."

Sean blinked. "No standard settings or reference points?"

Bill let out a dry chuckle. "You really think we've got time for that?"

There it was—the first crack in the system.

Sean nodded slowly. This wasn't just about slow die changes; it was about the mindset. They had accepted inefficiency as normal.

"Do you mind if we try something, Bill?" Sean asked, stepping closer.

Bill looked at him for a second, shook his head, and replied, "Why not? Apparently, you think you know more than me and my team?"

"Instead of adjusting blind, can we mark the ideal alignment points? So next time, you know exactly where to set it?"

The operator hesitated, glancing at Bill, who shrugged. "Give it a shot."

Sean turned to another operator. "Grab some marking tools."

Within minutes, they had tagged reference points on the die setup. When the next changeover happened, the setup time dropped from 45 minutes to 35.

Bill raised an eyebrow, impressed. "Huh, didn't think about that. Looks like maybe you've done this a time or two," he said.

Sean smiled. "Yes, sir—and thank you for being open to trying something new. I don't claim to know more than you or your team; I just asked a few questions and nudged you to look at it differently."

It was a small win, but it mattered. More importantly, it sent a message that just because something has always been done a certain way doesn't mean it should stay that way. Word would also spread—not that Sean was the kind of leader who forced change, but that he was the kind who listened, collaborated, went to where the employees were, and believed the people closest to the work—whether in a business, a school, a nonprofit, or even a family—often held the best ideas.

Meeting the Frontline Workers

As Sean continued to walk around the shop floor, he approached a group of workers packaging finished goods. "Morning, everyone. I'm Sean, a bald guy from Ohio, and I am here to help you build this into a place you love coming to every day. I'm here to work with you to figure out how we can make things better for all of us."

A woman in her mid-forties, Maria, crossed her arms. "Better how?"

Sean smiled. "That's a great question. The truth is, we need to make some changes to keep this company moving forward. But this isn't about making cuts or adding stress. It's about making improvements that help us all succeed. It's about creating a company we can all be proud of."

He paused, then added, "My job is to work with you to figure out what those changes should be. Because let's be honest—you're the ones who know how things run around here. You're the experts. I'm just the guy who showed up with a notebook and a title."

Maria raised an eyebrow. "So, what, you're here to 'partner' with us?"

Sean grinned. "That's the buzzword, right? 'Partnering with the workforce.' It's right up there with 'leveraging synergies' and 'moving the needle.'"

Maria smirked as she tried hard not to laugh out loud.

"I've read the HR manual," Sean said with a wide grin. "But no, I'm here to listen, ask too many questions, and probably get in your way until we make things better."

She tilted her head slightly. "Alright, then. Let me turn it around on you. You keep asking questions, what about you? Who are you, not professionally, but personally? What should I know about 'Sean' the person?"

Sean smiled, caught off guard—but in a good way. "Fair enough. But only if you go first."

Maria considered for a moment, then said, "I've got two kids—one just started high school, and the other thinks she runs the house. Spoiler alert: she does. I've been here fifteen years, and I love this place even though it drives me crazy sometimes. I make a mean lasagna, and I'm irrationally competitive in trivia games."

Sean nodded. "Lasagna and trivia; got it. You're officially the most intimidating person I've met so far."

Maria chuckled. "Your turn, boss."

"Well," Sean said, "I've got a wife who's way too patient with me, and a son who keeps trying to teach me TikTok dances that I'm physically incapable of doing. I'm a recovering Mountain Dew addict; I once bought a car without telling my wife—huge mistake—and I haven't missed a 5 a.m. workout in about five years. Mostly because I'm stubborn, not disciplined."

Maria laughed. "Mountain Dew? That explains everything."

"I know, right?" Sean said with mock seriousness. "Poor judgment and questionable taste—at least I'm consistent."

Maria shook her head, still smiling. "Well, you've got your work cut out for you."

"Story of my life," Sean said. "But I've learned that any place still full of people who care, even a little, is a place worth the effort."

Maria gave a small nod, the kind that said: *Alright. I'll give you a shot.*

And Sean knew from experience—that's all he needed.

Sean spent the next hour stopping by various stations, asking workers about their jobs, their frustrations, and their personal lives.

He circled back around to the press department and Bill and his team.

"I know we already met, but just curious—how long have you been here?" Sean asked.

"Thirty-two years," Bill replied with a hint of pride.

Sean nodded. "Thank you for your loyalty to Summit; you must know this machine better than anyone."

Bill shrugged. "I know it well enough to keep it running. It's temperamental, though. We've been asking for upgrades for years."

Sean and Bill ended up talking for another twenty minutes, the kind of conversation that flowed easily—not about strategy or metrics, but about the things that really mattered.

They talked about family, Bill sharing stories about his two grown kids and how his daughter had just landed her first real job out of college. Sean smiled, listening intently, asking questions that made it clear he wasn't just being polite, he genuinely cared. In return, Bill asked about Sean's wife, and Sean laughed as he described her uncanny ability to out-fish him every time they were out on the ocean.

That, of course, led to fishing.

Within minutes, they were trading stories about early mornings on quiet water, about the ones that got away, and about the gear they swore by. Sean mentioned the little cove he and Mary had found just a mile out in the ocean and how he and Mary always returned to—"never the same trip twice"—while Bill swore by a particular brand of topwater lure that, according to him, "ought to be illegal, it's so good."

It was the kind of connection that couldn't be forced. Just two men, one in boots and coveralls, the other in a polo and khakis, talking about life. No titles or hierarchy—just mutual respect and genuine curiosity about each other.

At one point, Bill chuckled and shook his head. "Never thought I'd be standing in a factory having a fishing talk with the CEO."

Sean smiled. "Well, I never thought I'd be getting fishing tips during a factory walk. Guess we're both full of surprises."

As they wrapped up, Bill thanked him again for stepping in earlier. Sean didn't make a big deal of it; he just thanked Bill for letting him help.

For Sean, that moment—two people connecting over work, life, and something as simple as a shared love for fishing—wasn't a distraction from leadership; it was leadership.

The Trust Piggy Bank

At lunchtime, Sean wandered into the breakroom, where a group of employees sat eating. He grabbed a bottle of water and gestured toward an empty chair. "Mind if I join you?"

The workers exchanged glances before Maria nodded. "Sure."

As he sat down, Sean asked the group what they thought was holding the company back.

Maria talked about how the team was stretched thin after a round of layoffs the previous year. Another worker, James, the warehouse supervisor, explained how the conveyor system had been breaking down more frequently, adding hours to their shifts.

"Why do you think it hasn't been fixed?" Sean asked.

James shrugged. "Management's been more worried about saving money than keeping things running smoothly."

Sean leaned forward. "I hear you," he said. "And I'm sorry it's been that way. That's not how it should be. My job is to help make this a place where you feel supported and where you have the tools you need to succeed."

"We've heard that before," Maria said flatly. Her tone made it clear that promises alone wouldn't win her over.

Sean nodded. "You're absolutely right," he said. "Words are cheap. Trust doesn't come from what I say, it comes from what I do."

He paused, then smiled. "Let me tell you how I think about trust. It's like a piggy bank. Every positive action I take—whether it's showing up, following through on a commitment, or treating you and this team with respect—is like making a deposit. Over time, those deposits add up, and trust grows." The room was quiet, everyone listening intently.

"But here's the thing about that piggy bank: withdrawals are easy. If I say one thing and do another—if I make promises I don't keep—

that's a withdrawal." Sean paused for a second, then continued. "The impact of a withdrawal is ten times that of a deposit. It's like at home with your husband, wife, or significant other. Those small things you do or say every day make deposits; that birthday or anniversary you forget, for example, is going to use up a lot of those deposits—if you know what I mean."

Sean leaned back, rubbing his bald head with a chuckle. "If I make too many withdrawals, I'll be overdrawn. And trust me, being overdrawn is a terrible feeling. Back in my early Army days, I wasn't great with my money. I'd blow my paycheck on dumb stuff and end up eating ramen noodles all week just to save enough for beer on the weekends."

The group cracked a few smiles, and Sean could feel the tension easing.

"I'm not going to tell you I'll never mess up, because I'm human, and I am going to make a lot of mistakes. But here's my promise: if I do make a withdrawal, I'll own it, and I'll work twice as hard to make it right."

Maria tilted her head slightly. "So, what's your first deposit?" she asked.

Sean grabbed a marker and wrote his cell phone number on the whiteboard in the breakroom. "If you've got ideas, concerns, or just want to chat, don't hesitate to reach out. Seriously: call or text me anytime. But I do have one favor to ask…"

41

The room quieted, a few people leaning in, curious.

Sean grinned. "Please, for the love of all things holy, no prank calls. Most nights I'm sitting alone in my corporate apartment, eating a microwave dinner that's somehow both frozen and lava, listening to a leadership podcast that just told me I should be journaling about gratitude. If you interrupt that with a knock-knock joke at 10 p.m., I might genuinely lose it. Don't be the reason I end up arguing with my toaster."

The room erupted in laughter, and Sean let the moment settle. This was how trust started—not with grand speeches, but with genuine moments of connection.

Chapter 6: Evaluate-Start with Why (ASSESS)

Sean had come to learn—both the hard way and the hilarious way—that meaningful change in any area of life starts with brutal honesty. Whether you're trying to fix a broken culture, repair a relationship, or just figure out why your kid suddenly doesn't want you to drop them off at school, you can't skip the assessment phase. You must start by telling the truth about where things stand. That's why his framework for change began with one word: **ASSESS.** It wasn't just a business acronym—it was a life skill.

The first "A" stood for **Articulate the Why**. If you couldn't clearly explain why something needed to change, you had no business asking anyone else to change. Sean had used this same approach whether he was launching a company-wide transformation or convincing his son Timmy that yes, brushing your teeth is still necessary—even on weekends.

Sean stood in front of a whiteboard in the conference room with a marker in hand—his first time wielding it in this new role. He hesitated for a second. "Alright," he said with a grin, "someone double-check me because if I spell this wrong, it's going to be a long day." A few chuckles rolled through the room as he slowly wrote five letters across the board:

A–S–S–E–S–S

"This isn't just a checklist," he told the group, underlining the word with theatrical flair. "It's our compass, and before we start making bold plans, fixing processes, or reorganizing anything, we have to get real about where we are right now." He turned back to the room. "That means no sugarcoating, no spin, no 'let's circle back.' Just the truth."

He paused, then added, "Because if you've ever tried to plan a vacation with your in-laws, you know what happens when people aren't aligned. The same thing happens in organizations, families, school boards, or group texts about potlucks—chaos."

The group laughed, but the point landed.

"Before we can communicate the 'why' to everyone else, we as a leadership team must be aligned on what it is. Otherwise, we're just giving people mixed messages and hoping they magically follow along." Sean tapped the board again. "So let's start with clarity, because if it's not clear to us, it won't be clear to them."

Facing Reality

David adjusted his glasses. "Alright, let's start with the basics."

Sean pulled out a report and handed out copies. "Here's what we know so far:

• Lead times have increased by 18% over the last two years.

• Defect rate is hovering at 7%—well above industry standards.

• Customer complaints about late deliveries have doubled in the past year."

Karen sighed. "No wonder our biggest accounts are getting antsy."

Marcus flipped through the numbers, frowning. "Our costs are climbing because we're throwing overtime at problems instead of fixing the root causes." He shook his head. "I've brought it up before, but no one wanted to slow down long enough to actually fix anything. They just wanted the fires put out."

"What about employee turnover?" Sean asked.

Marcus nodded grimly. "Worse than last year; people are either leaving for better pay or just getting fed up and leaving."

Ray leaned back in his chair, arms crossed. "So let me get this straight—we're behind on production, losing money, bleeding employees, and pissing off our customers. Great start."

"You forgot 'our equipment is outdated, our processes are inconsistent, and communication between departments is a mess,'" Sean said with a rhetorical smile.

Karen exhaled sharply. "And we wonder why morale is in the gutter?"

A heavy silence settled over the room. Sean let it hang for a moment. "I get it—this is overwhelming, but it's also fixable. We just need to be crystal clear on one thing before we move forward."

He turned back to the whiteboard and wrote:

Why are we doing this?

A Lesson from Outside the Office

Sean set the marker down. "Before we move another inch, we need to agree on the why. Knowing the why isn't just a business thing; it's the same in our personal lives."

He leaned against the table. "Years ago, I realized I was drinking too much. Always being on the road, alone in a hotel, away from my family, it was easy to slip into a routine that wasn't healthy. But until I understood *why*—why I needed to quit—it wasn't going to work. First, I realized that my wife, Mary, and my son Timmy deserved better. Even the organizations I worked with deserved better. Once I saw it that way, the change became non-negotiable." He paused, letting the room sit in the weight of the moment.

"Another time, Mary and I made the decision to move across the country for a new opportunity. It was exciting, but also scary. If we hadn't been crystal clear about why we were making that move, every little setback, bad day at work, or box that took months to unpack would have made us question whether it was worth it. The why was the anchor that kept us committed."

Marcus nodded. "So, you're saying we need that same anchor here?"

"Exactly," Sean said. "If we skip defining it, the first obstacle we hit will have people wondering if we should've even started."

Defining the Why

"If we don't clearly communicate the why behind this change, people will fill in the blanks themselves—and it won't be good. They'll assume we're cutting jobs or that this is just another short-term program that will fade away."

He paused. "We, as leaders, must get aligned on the why first. Once we do, we need to take the time to explain it to our teams, answer their questions, and keep repeating it."

Marcus was the first to respond. "So how do we make sure they get it? I mean, really get it. Because 'we need to be more efficient' isn't exactly inspiring."

"We repeat it constantly," Sean said. "Every meeting, every one-on-one, every casual conversation in the hallway. It can't just come from me; it must come from all of us. People believe what their direct leaders say more than what comes from the top."

David nodded. "So, we equip our frontline supervisors to tell the story too."

Karen raised her hand, smiling. "Before we start repeating anything, we need to be crystal clear on what our why actually is. We keep talking about change, but what's the deeper reason? Why should people care?"

Sean laughed softly. "You've caught me again, Karen. I have this tendency to get ahead of myself; sometimes I like the sound of my own voice a little too much."

Karen tilted her head with a grin. "Sometimes?"

The room chuckled, and Sean let the laughter linger before continuing. "Alright, guilty as charged. But here's the thing—leaders who only talk never listen. And if I'm honest, that's been a growth area for me.

"You're right, we can't just parrot messages until we've defined something worth repeating. So, let's pause here and do the harder work: figuring out our true why. Once we nail that, the how gets a lot easier."

Building the Why

Marcus broke the silence. "If we don't change, this company won't survive. That's the truth, isn't it?"

"It is," Sean agreed. "But survival alone isn't enough. Fear can motivate you, but it doesn't inspire you. What's the bigger purpose—what are we fighting for?"

Karen sat up. "People want to feel like their work matters. If they believe the changes will make their jobs easier, safer, or more meaningful, they'll buy in."

David leaned forward. "Let's be honest: our service levels have dropped. If we don't improve, our customers will leave. So part of our why must be delivering better for them."

Marcus added, "We also have a responsibility to our people. This isn't about squeezing every dollar in savings. If we do this right, we create stability, opportunity, and a company they can be proud of."

Ray shrugged. "That's fine, but most people care about themselves first. How does this help *them*?"

Sean nodded. "Then let's speak their language. If we succeed, what does it mean for them?"

David replied, "Better job security, less chaos, and fewer headaches dealing with broken processes."

Karen added, "It also means more chances to grow. Right now, people feel stuck."

Sean turned to the whiteboard. "Alright—why do we need to change?"

Karen spoke first. "We need stability. If this company doesn't turn around, none of us have jobs."

✓ **To ensure long-term stability, so people have secure jobs.**

David added, "But it's not just about keeping the doors open; we want this to be a place where people actually want to work."

✓ **To create a workplace where people can thrive, not just survive.**

Ray said, "We waste a ridiculous amount of time on things that shouldn't be this hard."

✓ **To continuously improve how we work, making it easier to succeed.**

David finished, "At the end of the day, we survive by serving our customers. If we don't get better, they'll go somewhere else."

✓ **To better serve our customers, so we remain competitive and grow.**

Sean stepped back. "This is our message. This is what we repeat over and over again. If someone asks why we're making changes, this is our answer."

Ray crossed his arms. "And what if they don't buy it?"

"Then we show them," Sean said. "Through action, not just words."

As the meeting wrapped up, Sean looked around the table. They had taken an important first step, but the real challenge lay ahead.

Change isn't just about new processes or cost savings; it's about shifting habits, mindsets, and priorities. Just like when you quit drinking, move to a new city, or make any big life change, success comes down to one thing: whether people are willing to keep doing the work long after the excitement of the change fades.

Chapter 7: Searching for Change Champions (A_SSESS)

Sean had spent the past several days immersing himself in the day-to-day operations, watching how people worked, how they communicated, and most importantly, who they listened to. He wasn't just looking for employees who were good at their jobs; he was searching for change champions. True change didn't happen through top-down mandates; it happened through influence. And influence didn't come from a title—it came from trust.

If this change was going to stick, Sean needed more than just leadership team buy-in. He needed the everyday experts, the ones in the trenches, solving problems and keeping things running—to believe in it. The same principle applied far beyond the workplace. If you want to run your first marathon, it's one thing for a coach to hand you a training plan. But it's something entirely different when a running buddy you respect invites you to join them for an early morning training run.

Think about learning a new skill. A YouTube tutorial might give you the steps, but it's the friend who's already done it successfully that convinces you it's possible. That's the kind of influence Sean was looking for.

At their next leadership meeting, Sean walked to the whiteboard and wrote a single question:

Who do people trust?

He turned to the group. "I want names. Not managers or people with the biggest titles. I'm talking about the informal leaders—the people others go to for advice, guidance, or just a reality check."

A pause followed as the team exchanged glances. Then, one by one, names began appearing:

• Bill – The veteran machine operator who knew the equipment inside and out. Rough around the edges, often skeptical, but trusted because he knew the work. If Bill bought in, others would follow.

• Maria – A floor lead who spoke her mind, called things as she saw them, and got things fixed when no one else could.

• James – A supervisor in the warehouse who kept his team calm and focused, even when chaos was at its peak.

Sean jotted each name down. He had already met all three during his daily walks and casual breakroom conversations.

Ray crossed his arms. "I still don't see why we need these so-called change champions when we already have a leadership team. That's our job."

Sean set the marker down. "Okay, let me ask you this—if you want to make a big life change, like starting a new diet, who are you more likely to listen to? A stranger on Instagram, or a close friend who's already lost the weight and kept it off?"

Ray hesitated.

"We set the vision," Sean continued, "but they determine if it actually happens."

He drew a simple diagram on the board, with Leadership on one side and Workforce on the other.

"There's always a gap between leaders and the people doing the work. The bigger the gap, the harder the change. Change champions help close that gap."

The Diffusion of Innovation Theory

Sean smiled. "I don't want to geek out too much, but this next bit explains exactly why this works." He wrote on the whiteboard:

Diffusion of Innovation Theory

"This comes from Everett Rogers, a sociologist who studied how new ideas spread. It's been built on by people like Malcolm Gladwell and Simon Sinek. The idea is that people adopt change at different rates."

He listed them on the board:

1. Innovators – First to try something new.

2. Early Adopters – Respected influencers who get others on board.

3. Early Majority – Join in once they see proof.

4. Late Majority – Wait until almost everyone else is doing it.

5. Laggards – Only change when they absolutely have to.

"Successful change," Sean explained, "isn't about forcing the majority to act. It's about inspiring the innovators and early adopters—the people others already trust. If they move first, the early majority will follow."

Marcus leaned forward. "So, our change champions are basically our innovators and early adopters?"

"Exactly," Sean said. "It's like when someone in your neighborhood starts a small garden in their front yard. At first, people are curious. A few months later, three more houses on the block are doing it. That's social proof—and it's powerful."

David spoke up. "So how do we pick the right people?"

Sean pointed to the names on the board. "We already have our shortlist. Now, I'll meet with them to explain what we're doing and why. But this isn't about appointing them—it's about enlisting them."

By the end of the day, Sean had meetings set with Bill, Maria, and James. If he could earn their trust, they would become the voice of the change.

Chapter 8: The Invitation

Sean sat across from Maria, James, and Bill in the breakroom. The hum of machinery and the faint clang of the press line drifted in through the walls, mixed with the unmistakable smell of burnt coffee that seemed like it had been brewing since the Reagan administration. Maria, James, and Bill didn't seem to mind; Sean felt lucky he wasn't a coffee man as he took a sip of his Celsius.

Maria leaned back in her chair, arms crossed. "So, let me get this straight. You're saying we're supposed to be… leaders?"

James chuckled. "Maria, you already are. Half the plant comes to you when something breaks down."

She shrugged. "Yeah, because management—no offense, boss—usually isn't listening."

Bill finally spoke up, his voice carrying the weight of three decades. "That's the real problem, isn't it? Thirty-two years here, I've seen more programs than I can count. Big speeches, new posters on the wall—and then nothing changes."

Sean leaned in, resting his arms on the table. "That's why I'm here talking to you three first. Not the managers, not the executives—you. Because people don't follow titles, they follow trust. When folks on the floor see you believe in something, they'll pay attention. That's how real change starts—through the people others already listen to."

Maria raised an eyebrow. "So, we're your guinea pigs?"

Sean grinned. "More like early adopters; you set the tone. If this works, others will join, not because I tell them to but because they see you doing it. That's how ideas spread. Same way a new app takes off, or how one neighbor puts up Christmas lights in November and suddenly the whole block looks like the North Pole."

James laughed. "So basically, we're the test pilots. If we crash, everyone else keeps their feet on the ground."

Sean took another sip of his Celsius. "Pretty much, but I don't think you'll crash. People already turn to you—for answers, for help, for guidance. That's leadership, whether you signed up for it or not."

Bill eyed him. "What if we think something's garbage?"

"Then you tell me," Sean said without hesitation. "Loudly—but preferably not yelling too loud at me."

That got a laugh from Maria and James, and even Bill cracked the hint of a smile. For the first time, Sean felt the door to change inching open. If these three believed, even cautiously, the rest of the plant might just follow.

James took a sip of his coffee. "Alright, but what if people don't listen to us? What if they push back?"

Sean nodded. "Some will, because let's face it—change is hard. But remember, people don't resist change; they resist being changed. They need to see it working, and they need to trust that it's real. The fact is, they'll trust you before they trust me."

Maria tilted her head. "Why's that?"

"Because you're in the trenches with them," Sean said simply. "They know you. They've seen you pull extra shifts, fight for better schedules, cover when someone is out sick. Trust is the currency of relationships, and you've earned their trust. I haven't—yet. Remember when I talked about the 'trust piggy bank' that day in the breakroom? You three have a lot of deposits in your banks, while I don't."

Bill grunted. "Trust is earned, alright… and it can be lost just as fast."

"That's why we're going to do this right. No quick fixes and no false promises—just real, sustainable change," Sean said. "Kind of like when someone decides they want to rebuild a strained friendship. You can't just say 'we're good now' and expect it to stick. It takes repeated, consistent effort over time before that trust comes back."

Maria snorted. "Patience isn't exactly my strong suit."

"Which is why I paired you with James," Sean said with a grin.

James laughed. "So, I'm here to keep Maria from scaring people off?"

Maria rolled her eyes. "Oh please, people love me."

Bill smirked. "They love you because you don't take crap from anyone."

Sean smiled. "That's exactly why I need you all in this."

The room was quiet for a moment. Sean could see the wheels turning in their heads.

Maria sighed dramatically. "Fine, but if this turns into some corporate nonsense, I reserve the right to call you out."

"Deal," Sean said without hesitation.

James grinned. "Alright, Sean, you've got us. Let's see if we can make a difference."

Bill, still the most skeptical, took a long sip of his coffee before finally nodding. "Alright, let's see if this time is different."

Sean leaned back in his chair, feeling the shift in the room. This was it—the beginning of the ripple effect. Leadership wasn't about standing at the top and giving orders; it was about building trust from the inside out, and it was already happening.

Chapter 9: Selecting One Place to Begin (AS<u>S</u>ESS)

Sean sat at the front of the conference room as his leadership team gathered around. David, Marcus, Karen, and Ray were there, along with the change champions—Maria, James, and Bill. This wasn't going to be a top-down decision. They needed alignment from both leadership and frontline influencers.

Sean walked to the whiteboard and wrote a single phrase in bold letters:

Where we start determines where we go.

"We're not flipping a switch across the entire organization," Sean said, writing the words **Start Small, Scale Smart** underneath. "We begin in one area, learn from it, refine our approach, and then scale to other parts of the business."

James leaned forward. "Why not just roll everything out at once? If we know where we want to go, why not get everyone moving at the same time?"

Sean nodded. "Good question. Think about it like hosting a massive family reunion. If you try to cook every single dish at once, you'll end up with half-cooked meals and burnt desserts. When we spread limited resources across too many places at once, no one gets what they need to succeed."

59

Maria smiled knowingly. "So instead of a full buffet, we serve one dish first, see how it goes, and make sure we get it right before rolling out the entire meal?"

"Exactly," Sean said. "When we try to do too much at once, we don't just risk failure—we almost guarantee it. When things get tough, people will go back to what's familiar, not because they're stubborn, but because we didn't give them enough clarity or support to stick with the new way."

He pointed to the board. "That's why we start in one place. Not because it's the only area that needs attention, but because we need to show what's possible. We go deep, not wide. We build momentum where it matters most—on the ground, with real people solving real problems."

Karen raised her hand. "But what about everyone else? Won't they feel left out?"

"They might," Sean admitted, "but they'll also get curious—and that's what we want. When one team starts seeing better results, stronger communication, and higher morale, others notice. They start asking questions, and they wonder, 'Why is their team running better than ours? What are they doing differently?'"

He smiled before continuing. "And curiosity is gold. If we do this right, we create a pull from the other departments."

"It's the same outside of work. Think about your neighborhood around the holidays. Nobody wants to be the first to put up Christmas lights in November, but once one house does, others follow and pretty soon the whole street is glowing. Or take youth sports—when one team starts showing up early, warming up together, encouraging each other from the sidelines, other teams notice and begin copying it. Nobody sent out a memo telling them to—it spreads because people don't want to be left behind when they see something working."

He tapped the table for emphasis. "That's the kind of pull we're after. Not forcing people into compliance, but sparking something so good, so obvious, that others can't help but want in."

David leaned back, nodding. "So instead of forcing it on everyone, we create a proof point. Something people can believe in."

"Exactly," Sean said. "We light one fire and let the sparks spread. It also gives us the chance to try things out in one department, learn from it, and adjust before spreading it to other departments."

Choosing Where to Start

Karen leaned forward. "So how do we pick the starting point?"

Sean wrote on the whiteboard:

Focus Creates Pull.

"We don't start with what's most broken. We start somewhere visible, somewhere connected to multiple parts of the organization so people can see the difference when things improve."

David shifted in his chair. "What if this works and people start lining up to be next? How do we keep from overextending?"

"That's why we set clear criteria for expansion," Sean said. He flipped to a new section of the whiteboard and wrote:

1. **Proven Results** – The first team must show measurable improvements before we scale.

2. **Employee Pull** – Other teams must request the change; we don't force it.

3. **Leadership Readiness** – Leaders in the next area must be prepared before we start.

Bill smiled. "So no just dumping a new system on people and hoping for the best?"

Sean chuckled. "Not unless we want to watch it crash and burn."

Making the Call

Maria leaned back. "So where do we start?"

James didn't hesitate. "Customer service."

A few heads turned. "Why them?" Karen asked.

James explained, "They touch almost every part of the business. If they improve, everyone feels it—customers, operations, even finance."

Marcus nodded. "They're also visible. People will notice if they start running smoother."

Sean pointed his marker at the team. "That's the pull effect in action. We're not selling change—we're proving it."

Building the Game Plan

Bill cracked his knuckles. "Alright, customer service it is. What's step one?"

Without hesitation Sean responded, "We talk to the team, watch how they work, and ask them what slows them down. We're not here to tell them what's broken—we're here to let them tell us."

Karen smirked. "You really believe in this 'listen before you fix' thing, huh?"

Sean laughed. "What can I say? People support change more when they feel heard."

Bill gave a small nod. "Alright, let's get to work."

Chapter 10: Evaluating Organizational Readiness (ASS<u>E</u>SS)

One morning, during the leadership huddle, Sean stood at the front of the room, gripping a list of questions. He had spent weeks walking the plant floor, listening to employees, meeting with department leaders, and observing how things worked—not how leadership thought they worked, but how they really operated day in and day out. Now, it was time to assess the company's true readiness for change.

He turned to the whiteboard and wrote three key categories:

1. **Continuous Process Improvement**
   • Do employees believe they have the ability to improve their own work, or do they see it as "just the way things are?"
   • When was the last time someone suggested an improvement that actually got implemented?
   • How much waste—time, materials, effort—do people see but feel powerless to address?

2. **Cultural Enablers**
   • How do employees feel about leadership? Do they trust them? Do they feel heard?
   • What's the team's appetite for change?
   • Are they burned out? Are they skeptical? Are they ready to try something new?

3. **Enterprise Alignment**

   • Do different departments see themselves as part of the same team, or do they operate in silos?

   • How well do employees understand the company's overall goals?

   • Are people working toward a shared vision, or are they just clocking in and out?

Sean turned back to the group. "We're not guessing here, we need real data. We're going to take a sample of employees—frontline workers, supervisors, middle management, even members of the leadership team—and ask questions that will help us understand how ready the organization is for what we are about to do. The goal isn't just to get answers, it's to listen."

The room fell silent as everyone processed what Sean was saying. Karen spoke up, "I thought we had already decided the change was going to happen and it wasn't optional?"

Sean nodded. "We did; this isn't about if we do it but how."

Ray, arms crossed as usual, let out a skeptical chuckle. "So, we are going to ask employees questions to gauge how ready they are for something we have already decided to do?"

David leaned forward. "I think what Sean is saying is the responses to the assessment will help us understand exactly how much work the change will take and some areas we need to focus on."

Sean nodded. "Exactly, it will also give us a baseline. We will know where we stand before the work begins, and then at least annually we do the assessment again to see how much progress we have made."

Maria chimed in. "More importantly, what are our biggest blockers? Who's going to resist just because they don't want to change? We need to know what we're walking into."

Karen raised an eyebrow. "So, basically… we're about to poke the bear?"

Sean smirked. "Yep, but better to poke the bear now than find out later that it's been asleep for years and doesn't want to wake up."

Bill chuckled. "You've got a hell of a way with metaphors, boss."

Sean set the marker down. "Look, we don't get to decide if people are ready; they do. All we can do is figure out where they stand, meet them where they are, and move forward with the ones who are willing."

Karen sighed, "alright let's find out what kind of bear we're dealing with."

Assessing Readiness: What We Learned

Over the next few days, Sean and his leadership team moved methodically through the organization, conducting interviews, observing daily operations, and gathering candid feedback. They met employees on their own turf—not in conference rooms, but on the shop floor, in break areas, and even in the parking lot at shift change.

Karen and Maria spent time with frontline workers, asking about their frustrations and what changes, if any, they believed could make their jobs easier. James and Marcus sat down with shift supervisors and middle management, probing into whether they felt equipped to lead through change—or if they were just bracing for the latest "flavor of the month" initiative.

Sean even made a point to speak with longtime employees one-on-one, particularly those who had seen change initiatives come and go over the years. He wanted to hear their raw, unfiltered thoughts. And they didn't hold back. By the end of the assessment, the team had collected dozens of pages of notes, observations, and insights.

The Debrief

The leadership team gathered in the conference room for the big debrief. Sean stood at the front, flipping through the summary of findings. The energy in the room was a mix of curiosity and unease.

"Alright," Sean started. "We asked, we listened, and now it's time to face reality. We took all the responses, quantified each one, compiled themes, and the following are the high-level findings."

He clicked the remote and a slide lit up on the projector with three major themes.

Maria immediately leaned back in her chair, smirking. "Wait… are my eyes deceiving me, or did Sean just trade in his precious whiteboard for PowerPoint?"

James grinned. "Unbelievable. I thought the man would rather eat cafeteria meatloaf than open a slide deck."

Bill shook his head slowly. "Somewhere, a dry-erase marker just cried."

The room chuckled, and Sean rolled his eyes. "Very funny, I just figured I'd switch things up today; let the computer do a little work and give the dry erase board a break."

Maria tapped her pen against her notebook. "Oh no, no. This is history in the making. We should document this moment: *Sean actually using technology instead of scribbling dramatic words in all caps on a whiteboard.*"

James smirked. "Quick, somebody take a picture before he goes back to writing 'TRUST' across the wall in giant letters."

"Or 'DON'T SCREW IT UP,'" Bill added, grinning.

Sean held up a hand. "For the record, I do not have a monopoly on dramatic whiteboard moments. Ok, let's take a look at what we have here.

1. The Good: People Want Things to Get Better
Sean scanned the room. "Let's start with the positive—most

employees actually want change. They're frustrated, yes, but not because they're against improvement. They're tired of inefficiencies, of workarounds, and of problems being ignored."

Maria nodded. "One of the press operators told me, "If you actually fix the stuff we complain about every day, we'll back you all the way. But if this turns into another round of meetings that go nowhere, don't waste our time.'"

David leaned forward. "I heard the same thing from the supervisors. They aren't against us, they just don't want to waste energy on something that won't last." Sean nodded. "That's huge. It means we don't have to sell them on the idea of improvement; we just have to prove it's real."

2. The Bad: Deep Skepticism
Sean clicked to the next slide. "But then, there's this deep systemic skepticism."

Karen sighed. "Yeah. I talked to a few guys who have been here twenty-plus years. They've seen this before and flat-out told me, 'Leadership always talks big, but nothing ever really changes.'"

Ray crossed his arms. "I mean… can you blame them? Look at the track record."

Marcus glanced at the notes. "This isn't just skepticism; it's a trust problem. People don't trust leadership to follow through."

Sean exhaled. "That's exactly it, the lack of trust is the single biggest barrier to making this stick. Unfortunately, trust isn't built through memos and speeches; it's built through action."

3. The Ugly: Resistance Exists in the Middle

Sean clicked to the final point. "The biggest resistance isn't coming from the frontline," he said. "It's coming from middle management."

Karen frowned. "Why?"

David answered before Sean could. "Because they feel caught in the middle. They're expected to hit production targets, but now we're asking them to change the way they work. Let's be honest; some of them don't have the skills or confidence to lead change."

Maria sighed. "One of the supervisors told me, "I've been managing the same way for ten years, if this fails leadership won't get blamed. That tells me they're afraid of what happens if they get this wrong."

Sean nodded. "Fear leads to resistance. Not outright defiance, but slow, passive resistance. The kind that kills change quietly."

James leaned back. "So, what do we do about it?"

The Path Forward

Sean took a deep breath, looking around the room. "We've got the data. Now, we turn it into action."

"How do we measure if it's working?" Marcus asked.

"We track the same three things we assessed," Sean said. He switched to the whiteboard and wrote:

1. **Process Improvement** – Are employees actually seeing change in how they work? Are processes getting better? Are they being empowered by their leaders to make suggestions on improvements?
2. **Cultural Enablers** – Is trust in leadership increasing? Are supervisors engaging in the right behaviors?
3. **Enterprise Alignment** – Are different departments working toward a shared goal, or are they still siloed?

"We baseline where we are now," Sean continued, "and we check back in 90 days. If those three indicators aren't improving, we adjust." David smirked. "And if they are?"

"Then we know we're on the right path," Sean said. "More importantly, so will they." The team exchanged looks, knowing the next steps wouldn't be easy. But it felt like they weren't just talking about change, they were building it.

Chapter 11: Selecting Key Performance Indicators (KPIs) (ASSE<u>S</u>S)

The hum of phones, keyboards, and low chatter filled the customer service area as Sean and the leadership team stepped into the large room. This wasn't the press department where heavy machinery clanged and roared—it was quieter, but no less important. This was where customer frustration either got solved or got worse. If change was going to ripple outward, this was the place to start.

Employees glanced up as the group entered, curiosity sparking.

Maria whispered, "See, everyone's watching."

Sean smiled and nodded. "Exactly. If we get this right, people will notice. If we don't, they'll notice that too."

He gathered the leadership team, change champions, and a few customer service reps around a large mobile whiteboard they had wheeled into the corner. In bold letters, he wrote:

We can't improve what we don't measure.

"Here's the deal," Sean said. "If we're serious about making change stick, we can't rely on gut feelings or stories. We need measurable data. But the trick is that the data must matter to all of you who do the work every day—the subject matter experts. It's not about what the leadership team thinks."

He turned to one of the reps, a young guy named Alex who was juggling three blinking phone lines and a notepad filled with scribbles.

"Alex, what's the most frustrating part of your day?"

Alex leaned back in his chair, letting out a breath. "Honestly, it's hold times. Customers get cranky, and then we get cranky. Half the battle is just calming people down before we can even solve their problem."

Sean nodded and wrote on the board: **Hold Time – Customer Experience Impact.**

"Good, that's a leading indicator. If hold times drop, satisfaction goes up. Simple, clear, and visible."

Maria pointed to another rep, Denise, who was sipping coffee between calls. "What about you?"

Denise shrugged. "Follow-ups. We promise callbacks, but with so many cases in the queue, it's easy for things to slip. Customers hate it when we don't follow through."

Bill chimed in with a grin. "So basically, you want a KPI that's the equivalent of my wife asking, 'Did you actually take the trash out, or did you just say you would?'"

The group laughed, and Sean added to the board: **Follow-Up Completion Rate.**

"Perfect example," he said. "Accountability is about follow-through, whether it's trash at home or tickets at work."

Another rep, Jasmine, raised her hand. "Here's one that matters to us: first-call resolution. If we can solve a customer's issue right away instead of bouncing them around, it saves time and stress for everyone."

Karen leaned forward, nodding. "That's gold, not just because it helps customers, but it also shows whether our training and systems are working."

Sean circled the phrase: **First-Call Resolution.**

"These are the kinds of metrics that tell us if change is sticking where it matters most. They're not abstract; they're tied to daily work."

He stepped back so the whole group could see the list:

✓ Hold Time

✓ Follow-Up Completion Rate

✓ First-Call Resolution

"These are yours," Sean said, gesturing to the board. "You came up with them. That's how we create pull for what we start here—and hopefully spread across the company. When these numbers improve, everyone will see the results and want to know what's different here."

Alex smirked. "So basically, we get to be the guinea pigs?"

Sean grinned. "No, you get to be the pioneers. And when the rest of the company starts asking what's working, you'll be the ones they come to for answers."

Denise raised her coffee. "Then let's make sure we give them something worth copying."

The group laughed, and Sean could feel the shift. This wasn't just about KPIs anymore; it was about ownership. The team wasn't being told what to track; they were deciding it together. That difference—ownership instead of compliance, doing it with them instead of to them—was what would make the change stick.

Sean uncapped his marker again and wrote at the top of the board:

How We Stay Accountable

- Weekly leadership huddles – discuss KPIs and roadblocks.
- Visual management boards – visible to all employees.
- Daily huddles – adjust strategies based on results.

He stepped back. "These aren't just for leadership; they're for everyone. Visibility builds trust, and when the numbers are public, the conversation shifts from 'Why didn't management tell us?' to 'What are we going to do about it?'"

Ross, one of the reps who had been quiet until now, raised an eyebrow. "What if these numbers get worse before they get better?"

Sean shrugged. "Then we know we're changing things. Disruption isn't always comfortable or a straight line, but it's necessary. If your workouts don't make you a little sore, you're probably not getting stronger. It's the same principle here."

Karen smiled. "Alright—we track it, own it, and fix it fast."

Marcus leaned back in his chair, grinning. "No pressure, right?"

Maria jumped in. "If it works, Sean owes us a steak dinner."

Bill laughed and slapped the table. "Forget steak. I'll take ribs."

Sean chuckled, shaking his head. "Fine, deal. But first, let's earn it."

The room buzzed with laughter and a sense of shared purpose. For the first time in all the change initiatives Summit had done over the years, accountability didn't feel like something being imposed from above. It felt more like a commitment they were making to each other.

Chapter 12: Skill Up Through Training and Resourcing *(ASSESS)*

Sean knew they had laid a strong foundation. The leadership team was aligned, the why had been clearly defined, and key performance indicators (KPIs) were in place. But there was one undeniable truth he needed to reinforce—and he wanted to do it where the work happened.

He stood near the break room, Celsius in hand, while the leadership team gathered around a table that had seen more lunch debates than leadership discussions.

"We can't expect people to improve if we don't train them and give them what they need."

Marcus crossed his arms. "Alright, I hear you. But let's be real, this company has never been big on training, and we don't have unlimited time or money. What exactly are we talking about here?"

Sean pulled a dry-erase marker from his pocket and wrote two words on the portable board they kept near the vending machines:

Skills & Tools

"Every job here has two components," Sean explained. "The skills to do the job well, and the tools to do it efficiently. If we don't invest in both, we're setting people up to fail." He paused, letting it sink in. "But it goes deeper than that. If we're not willing to invest in our people—develop their capabilities, remove the obstacles that frustrate them—then we shouldn't expect them to invest in us."

He looked around the group. "People notice where leadership puts its time, money, and attention. If all we focus on is output, they'll give just enough to get by. But when they see we care about their growth—when we build them up instead of burning them out—that's when commitment kicks in. That's when they take ownership."

Building a Training Plan

Sean gathered the supervisors to join the leadership team and change champions. He listed three focus areas on the whiteboard:

1. **Leadership Training** – equipping supervisors to coach and solve problems.

2. **Process Training** – teaching people to work smarter, not harder.

3. **Technical Training** – making sure operators fully understand their tools and processes.

"Leadership training for who?" Maria asked.

"For every supervisor and manager," Sean said. "A lot of people here were promoted because they were good at their jobs, but no one taught them how to lead. I know, because I've been that person."

Bill chuckled. "Here comes another Army story."

Sean grinned. "Oh, it's a good one. I was 21 years old and stationed in Germany. One day I'm just one of the guys, the next I'm in charge of four of my closest friends due to getting promoted. I got a little bit of training, but not much coaching. I was expected to just 'figure it out.' I swung between being everybody's buddy and the guy barking orders; it was a mess."

The group laughed, but Sean's voice softened. "Years later, one of those guys told me, 'You cared, Sean—you just didn't know how to lead.' That stuck with me. You can be the most skilled person in the room as well as the most caring, but if no one's ever shown you how to influence, build trust, and bring people with you, you'll struggle. Promoting someone without preparing them is like handing over the keys to a race car and saying, 'Figure it out on lap one.'"

The 20–60–20 Human Behavior Model

Later that afternoon, Sean joined Marcus, David, and Maria at one of the workstations for a quick walk-through. In between machines running, he grabbed a marker and sketched three sections on the corner of the department's whiteboard:

- **20% – Elite Performers**

- **60% – Core Workforce**

- **20% – Underperformers**

"This is the 20–60–20 Model," Sean explained. "It's everywhere: leadership, sports, schools—anywhere people perform."

He tapped the top section. "About 20% are elite performers. They'll excel no matter what." Then he pointed to the bottom. "Another 20% are struggling—not always because they're incapable, but often because they're frustrated, because the system has worn them down."

Maria frowned. "Frustrated how?"

Sean leaned against the bench. "Think about when someone joins a gym. They start motivated, but if the equipment's broken, no one explains the exercises, and the classes are always full, they stop showing up. Same concept with our team members. If we don't remove the barriers, even good folks lose interest."

David nodded. "So, some of that bottom 20% could bounce back?"

Sean smiled. "Exactly. But the key is the 60% in the middle. They often follow the culture. If it's strong, they rise, but if it's weak, they coast. Our job is to create an environment where the middle moves up."

"So, we use the top 20%?" Marcus asked.

"Bingo," Sean said. "We give them responsibility, not just recognition. We let them coach, set the tone, and model what good looks like. When the middle 60% see respected peers leading the way, it's more powerful than anything we can put in an email."

The Turning Point

That Friday, Sean was walking past the shipping area when Bill waved him over.

"Got a minute?" he asked, leaning on a pallet jack. "Been thinking about a way to cut our changeover time. I think it could save us hours each week."

Sean smiled. "Bill, I've got all the time in the world for that; show me."

They walked through the process together, and Bill explained his idea. It wasn't just about going faster, it was about reducing frustration, smoothing the flow, and making everyone's day easier. Sean realized Bill wasn't just doing his job anymore, he was owning it. That was a sign the change they were working on together was starting to take hold

Chapter 13: Addressing Resistance and Strengthening Accountability

Sean had known from the beginning that turning around Summit would not be easy, it never was. Progress was rarely a straight line, and he expected challenges. But he wasn't prepared for the conversation he was about to have, one that would force him to make a tough decision that could either solidify or unravel the momentum they had built.

A Pattern of Resistance

From the start, Sean had been noticing signs of resistance from Ray, the Director of Operations. While other leaders had embraced the transformation with cautious optimism, Ray seemed unwilling—or unable—to engage fully. He consistently arrived late to the morning huddles, provided vague updates when asked about his department's progress, and continuously made sarcastic comments that undercut the team's momentum.

At first, Sean approached the situation with subtle redirection, using techniques he had learned from the Accountability Dial, a framework designed to progressively address performance and behavior issues. The framework emphasizes starting with subtle cues to address concerns and escalating only as necessary.

The first step, *The Mention,* was simple enough. Sean casually commented on Ray's behavior in a low-stakes way.

"Hey, Ray, I noticed you were a little late to the huddle this morning. Is everything okay?"

Sean framed it as a light inquiry, giving Ray space to acknowledge the issue and self-correct.

But Ray barely glanced at him and muttered, "Just had things to manage, not a big deal."

No meaningful change followed the brief conversation. As the weeks went on and the resistance became harder to ignore, Sean knew it was time to move to the next step in the Accountability Dial: *The Invitation.* This step wasn't about confrontation; it was about clarity. It involved shifting from casual observations to a more direct, intentional conversation. It was Sean's way of saying: *"I see what's happening, and I'm inviting you to own it—and I'm here to work together to fix it if needed."*

Over the years, Sean had learned that avoidance never led to alignment. But charging in too strong, too fast, only created defensiveness. The Invitation was about surfacing the issue without triggering a shutdown.

During one of their regular check-ins, Sean leaned forward slightly and said, "Ray, I wanted to get your perspective on how the transformation is going. Is there anything that's frustrating you or making it hard to engage?"

Ray didn't answer right away. He shifted in his seat, then smirked and leaned back, arms crossing tighter across his chest.

"It's fine," he said, voice flat. Not angry, not open—just guarded.

Sean nodded slowly, letting the silence hang for a moment. "Fine" wasn't the truth, not even close. But Sean didn't press—not yet. The Invitation wasn't about cornering someone; it was about planting a seed, and sometimes the most powerful leadership move was knowing when to leave space for that seed to take root.

He looked Ray in the eye—not with judgment, but with curiosity. "Okay. I appreciate you saying that," he said calmly. "If anything shifts, or if there's something I need to hear from your perspective, I hope you'll tell me. You've been here longer than most, and your voice carries weight. If something's getting in the way of you being all-in on this effort, I'd rather understand it than assume."

Ray didn't say anything, but Sean noticed a small flicker behind the mask. Just for a moment, the wall dipped. He wasn't ready to talk, but he had heard Sean. Sometimes that was enough to move the needle.

Sean knew that change didn't happen through one big breakthrough. It happened in small, steady steps. Conversations like this—respectful, firm, intentional—were the quiet turning points most people never noticed. But they were extremely important when trying to bring about change.

As the meeting wrapped, Sean jotted a quick note in his notebook: **Ray—Invitation extended, door is open. Watch for response.**

Unfortunately, the resistance only escalated. It wasn't explosive; it was quieter than that, but no less damaging. At one morning huddle, as another manager excitedly shared a recent win—reduced scrap rates on the second shift thanks to a new visual management board—Ray chuckled under his breath. It wasn't loud enough to cause a scene, but just loud enough to be heard by the people standing nearby. Sean knew it wasn't just a chuckle; it was a dismissal. A signal that success didn't matter, that it was a waste of time—or worse, fake enthusiasm for a change effort he didn't believe in.

Sean watched as the manager's voice wavered slightly, the energy draining from what had started as a proud update. A few team members exchanged glances and the air shifted. One small moment, but it landed hard.

Then came the press department meeting. The team had gathered to brainstorm solutions for a chronic bottleneck issue, something that had cost them hundreds of hours in lost time and was on the radar of nearly every department that relied on that process. Ideas were flowing from everyone in the meeting—minor layout changes, cross-training, and revised changeover procedures. Everyone was participating, except at the end of the table, where Ray sat with his arms folded, face blank, saying nothing.

It wasn't that he disagreed—he didn't engage at all. No questions, feedback, or suggestions. Just silence, laced with visible disapproval. *I don't believe in this. I'm not bought in. And I'm not going to pretend that I am.*

Sean knew what was happening. Ray wasn't just resisting change—he was quietly undermining it. Not in a dramatic way, but in the way that creates doubt. In the way that tells others it's safer to hold back than to step forward. That kind of passive resistance, especially from a respected voice, was often more contagious than open rebellion. Sean knew it was time to turn the dial again.

Addressing the Resistance Head-On

Sean realized it was time to move to *The Boundary,* the next level of the Accountability Dial. This phase was about clarifying expectations and consequences and ensuring there was no ambiguity about what needed to change. Later that afternoon, Sean invited Ray into his office for a one-on-one discussion.

"Ray," Sean began, his tone calm but firm, "I've noticed some patterns over the past several weeks—the same ones we've discussed before: showing up late to huddles, disengaging during meetings, and making comments that seem to undermine the team's efforts. I need to understand what's going on, because these behaviors are having an impact on the team."

Ray shifted in his chair, his expression unreadable. "I'm just doing my job."

Sean nodded. "I hear you, but being part of this team isn't just about tasks. It's about contributing to the culture we're building. Right now, what I'm seeing doesn't align with the direction we're heading. I want to understand if there's something we need to address together, or if this is more about whether you feel aligned with this transformation and the direction we are going as a leadership team and organization."

Ray's smirk faded slightly, but his skepticism remained. "I've been through these changes before," he said. "It never lasts and I'm not going to waste my time on something that's going to fall apart in six months."

Sean leaned forward. "I get it, Ray. You've been here a long time, and you've seen leaders come and go. But this isn't about the past; it's about what we can build for the future. Together, as a team, we have a chance to go in a new direction and create an organization we can all be proud of."

Ray crossed his arms. "And what if I don't think this direction is the right one?"

The Accountability Moment

Sean leaned forward, his voice low but firm. "Then we need to have a serious conversation about whether this is the right place for you, Ray."

There was no anger in Sean's tone—but there was edge. Controlled, measured frustration from a leader who had extended more patience than most would have. Sean had spent weeks listening, inviting, coaching, and giving every opportunity for alignment.

"I've been patient," Sean continued. "I've respected your history here and I've asked for your perspective, brought you into the process, and given you room to find your footing. But this isn't about you or me—it's about the 300 people counting on us to get this right."

He gestured toward the plant where most of the employees he was referencing worked.

"The rest of the leadership team is aligned. They've committed and are doing the hard work to bring about the change we need. This direction we're going—it's not optional. Not because I say so, but because the status quo is broken. And if we don't change, we don't survive."

Ray didn't speak. His eyes narrowed slightly, but the usual resistance in his body language wavered.

Sean held his gaze. "If you're not willing to engage fully, it's not fair to the rest of the team—or to you—to stay in a role where you're not aligned with where we're headed. I'm not asking for blind agreement, but I am asking for commitment. If that's something you can't offer, we need to be honest about that."

A long silence followed. Tension filled the air.

Finally, Ray said, more quietly than before, "I'll think about it."

Sean nodded, his tone softening slightly. "Good. I want you to. You've been a great asset to this company, Ray. You've seen things most of us haven't, and your experience matters. But if you choose to stay, I'm going to hold you to the same standards as everyone else. Not because I don't value you—but because I do. And because our people deserve consistency from their leaders."

He let the words settle. The moment was heavy, but necessary. Sean knew this wasn't just about Ray anymore; it was a message to the entire leadership team. This transformation was real, and from here on out, accountability wouldn't be implied—it would be expected.

The Decision

A few days later, Ray submitted his resignation. In his exit conversation, he admitted that he wasn't ready to embrace the changes Sean was leading.

"It's not you," he said. "I just don't think I have it in me to go through another transformation."

Sean thanked him for his honesty, but the departure was bittersweet. Losing a senior leader during a critical phase of the change was a setback, but Sean knew it was the right decision. Allowing Ray's disengagement to continue would have undermined the culture of accountability and commitment the team was working so hard to build.

Sean addressed it openly with his leadership team, reinforcing that what they were trying to do required full commitment. With Ray's departure, a new chapter began—one built on trust, alignment, and an unshakable commitment to progress

Chapter 14: Execution: Framing Clear Expectations and Objectives (FOCUS)

The team filed into what used to be one of the company's drab conference rooms. The long mahogany table was gone, replaced with open space, rolling chairs, and whiteboards lining every wall. Each wall had its own header in bold block letters: **Safety, Quality, On-Time Delivery, Cost, Productivity, Engagement.** Colored tape created neat sections, each one waiting to be filled.

Maria stopped just inside the doorway, eyes scanning the walls. "Oh no, they've multiplied."

Sean looked up from a stack of markers. "Multiplied?"

"Whiteboards," she said, pointing. "They're everywhere; it's like you let them breed."

David smirked. "This isn't an Obeya—it's a shrine to dry erase."

Marcus shook his head in mock disbelief. "I'm telling you, Sean, one day you're going to move into a house where every wall is just a giant whiteboard. The kitchen, the bathroom—hell, even the ceiling."

Bill grinned. "I bet that's how he proposed to Mary; he just wrote *Will You Marry Me?* in big block letters, circled it twice, and stood there with a marker."

Maria laughed. "Yeah, and then they probably picked their wedding date off a calendar he drew in the corner."

David pointed toward the wall labeled Engagement. "I'm guessing that's how you named your son too—drew up a whole fishbone diagram until *Tommy* floated to the top."

Sean raised an eyebrow. "You comedians done, or should I just go ahead and schedule the roast for next Friday?"

Bill shrugged. "Hey, you started it, boss, when you weaponized whiteboards."

Sean grinned. "Laugh all you want, but you're looking at the new nerve center for how we execute. No more chasing problems in ten different places. From now on, everything that matters is going to live here in plain sight."

Bill glanced at the headers. "So, each wall is one of our core metrics?"

"Exactly," Sean said. "Safety, Quality, On-Time Delivery, Cost, Productivity, and Engagement. These are the big levers that will move the business. If it doesn't tie to one of these, it's not getting our focus right now."

Karen crossed her arms. "So, we write all the things we need to work on improving on the whiteboard with a marker?"

"No," Sean said, tapping the marker against his palm and holding up a blank sheet. "It goes on an A3." He paused, then explained. "An A3 is just a structured way to solve a problem—one page. We write down the problem, the data, the root cause, and the plan for fixing it. If it's important enough to fix, it's important enough to document, analyze, and track. Initially we may only know the problem, but then as we work to fix issues we gather and document the rest of it. Then that A3 gets posted on the wall under the metric it supports. If it's a safety issue, it goes on the Safety wall. If it's about on-time delivery, it goes on that wall. Same with Quality, Cost, Productivity, and Engagement."

Bill raised an eyebrow. "So, it's basically homework for grown-ups?"

Sean smiled. "I had never thought of it that way, but I guess so. Think of it like this: it's not about paperwork, it's about clarity. If you've ever tried to lose weight, and you just said, *I want to get healthier,* that's too vague and chances are you'll never stick to it. But if you write down: *Current state: eating fast food three times a week. Goal: cook dinner at home four nights a week. Action plan: shop on Sunday, prep meals, and walk 20 minutes a day,* suddenly it's real. You've documented the problem and the steps, and you can track whether it's working."

Maria leaned forward, nodding. "So, the A3 is like a fitness tracker for problems."

"Exactly," Sean said. "It keeps us honest. Without it, we just say we're going to fix things, but then they get lost in the noise. With an A3, it's written down, owned by someone, tied to a bigger goal, and visible to the entire team."

He looked around the room, his tone more serious. "If it doesn't make it onto these walls, it doesn't get worked on unless it's part of day-to-day operations. That way, we're not chasing a hundred little distractions; we're focusing on the problems that actually move the needle."

He pointed around the room as he spoke, making the connection between those in the room and the work that would go on the whiteboards.

"This way, every improvement effort is tied directly to a result we actually care about—and everyone can see. No more pet projects just because someone yelled the loudest or has been here the longest. If it's not tied to a metric and it's not on the wall, it doesn't get worked on, unless it's just day-to-day operational stuff that keeps the place running."

Bill raised an eyebrow. "So, no more secret side projects?"

"Exactly," Sean said. "If it's not here, it's invisible, and if it's invisible, it's probably not worth our time right now."

Maria smirked. "So, we're basically putting our dirty laundry on display for the whole company?"

Sean shook his head. "Nope, we're putting our problem-solving muscle on display. Obeya isn't about shaming, it's about alignment and transparency. Everyone knows the priorities and sees what we are working on and the progress of each. If something stalls or needs help, it's visible and we can help."

Marcus walked over to the Productivity wall, tapping one of the blank A3 spaces. "So, who gets to put stuff up here?"

"Anyone," Sean said. "Leaders, change champions, frontline team members. If they see a problem worth solving, they fill out an A3 and give it to their leader, who brings it up here. Each week, as a team, we meet here and go over what's on the wall."

Maria walked over to the Cost wall and grabbed a marker. "First A3: reduce excessive marker purchases for Sean's whiteboard obsession."

The room burst into laughter.

Sean chuckled, shaking his head. "Fine, but I expect that one to show a positive ROI."

Karen smiled. "I like it, Sean. It's visual, focused, and it makes it hard for anyone to hide from what's actually happening."

"That's the point," Sean said. "We're not managing change from behind closed doors anymore. This is how we make execution visible and unavoidable."

Sean glanced toward the doorway. "Speaking of which, I've got someone here to help us kick this off."

A line leader named Tony stepped into the room, a little hesitant but holding a single-page A3 with notes scribbled in the margins. He looked around at the sea of leadership faces. "Uh… morning."

"Don't worry, Tony," Sean said with a grin. "This isn't *Shark Tank* and nobody's getting voted off the island. You're here to walk us through your idea so we can make it better together."

Marcus leaned over to Bill and whispered just loud enough for Tony to hear, "I think Sean's just excited he gets to use another whiteboard today."

Bill smirked. "Yeah, I bet Tony's A3 ends up on three different walls before we leave."

Sean shot them both a look. "Alright, comedians, let's focus. Tony—tell us what you've got."

Tony took a breath. "Okay, so we've been having a recurring safety issue with loose parts spilling out of bins in the assembly area. They end up on the floor, and people have tripped—no serious injuries yet, but it's only a matter of time."

"Good," Sean said, nodding toward the Safety wall. "Right away, we know where it belongs. Now walk us through your 'Current State' box on the A3."

Tony glanced down at his sheet of paper. "Currently, we're using shallow bins stacked on rolling carts. When the carts are moved, parts shift around and spill out. I've measured it and we lose about ten minutes every time someone has to stop and clean it up."

"Perfect," Sean said. "Clear facts, no drama. Now, what's your target condition?"

Tony straightened up a bit. "Within the next two weeks, all small parts will be stored in deeper, lidded bins with foam inserts to keep them in place. That should eliminate spills and cut cleanup time to zero."

Maria raised her hand. "Have you looked into whether we can standardize the bin size so they're interchangeable between carts?"

Tony nodded. "Yep, I talked to purchasing already and they said it's doable and only about $300 for the whole department."

Sean smiled and tapped the Safety wall. "That's the power of the A3—clear problem, clear solution, tied directly to a measurable result. We post it here, track it, and two weeks from now we'll review. If it works, we lock it in as standard work. If not, we adjust."

Bill raised an eyebrow. "So basically, we're not just fixing stuff, we're making sure the fix sticks."

"Exactly," Sean said. "The beauty of this system is that the best ideas aren't coming from this room; they're coming from the people doing the work. Our job is to remove barriers, give them the tools, and make sure every improvement connects to the results we care about."

Tony smiled, clearly more comfortable now. "So… does this mean my A3 passes?"

Sean grinned. "Not only does it pass, but it also goes up on the wall today. When it's done, we're going to celebrate the win, so people see what's possible."

As Tony put his A3 under the bold Safety header, Marcus muttered, "There it is—Sean's first official whiteboard victory in the new Obeya. Better take a picture before he adds glitter or something."

The room laughed, but the point was made; this wasn't about whiteboards—it was about creating a living, breathing visual system where the right work stayed visible, the right people stayed involved, and the right results stayed in focus.

Chapter 15: Optimizing Change Management through Training and Support *(FOCUS)*

Change doesn't fail because of bad ideas; it fails because of poor execution. You can have the most inspiring vision, the most innovative tools, or the most talented people, and still fall short if you don't equip them with the clarity, training, and support they need to adapt. Without those things, even the best intentions will get lost in confusion, resistance, and misalignment.

Sean had seen this play out in every kind of environment; businesses, schools, volunteer organizations, even personal goals. People would launch new initiatives with energy and optimism, only to watch momentum fade when reality set in. It wasn't usually because the plan was bad. More often, it was because no one had thought through how to engage people daily, guide them through the hard parts, and help them build new habits that would last.

But this time was different. His leadership team was united, his change champions were energized, and there was no silent waiting for the plan to fail. They were all committed, and that meant they could focus on execution the right way.

Sean stood at the front of the room with his leadership team and change champions gathered around. Marker in hand, he turned toward the whiteboard.

"Our job isn't just to tell people what's changing; it's to make sure they have the skills, confidence, and resources to thrive in the new system."

Building the Plan for Execution

Karen leaned forward. "So, where do we start?"

Sean wrote on the board:

1. Training That Works in the Real World

"Training needs to be practical, relevant, and embedded in the real work—or real life—it supports," he explained. "No one learns from sitting through an endless slideshow and hoping it sticks."

Maria grinned. "Thank God."

Bill chuckled. "If I have to sit through another policy lecture pretending it's 'training,' I'm making that prank call we talked about."

Sean smirked. "That's why we're moving to micro-trainings—five to ten-minute coaching sessions that focus on real situations, real fixes, and real-time feedback."

Marcus raised an eyebrow. "Training in what, exactly?"

"It depends," Sean said. "One day it might be teaching a team how to handle a tough customer conversation without escalating, while another day it might be walking a supervisor through filling out a visual management board. The principle is the same—keep it short, relevant, and directly tied to the outcome we want."

Marcus nodded. "So, no more one-and-done?"

"Not if we want it to stick," Sean said. "Repetition is how habits form. We're not training for head knowledge; we're training for muscle memory."

James spoke up. "Leadership needs to be part of it, right? Not just watching?"

Sean wrote on the board:

2. Leaders as Coaches, Not Enforcers

"Exactly," he said. "Leadership means being in the middle of the action, guiding and coaching, not hiding in an office reviewing reports. If we want people to embrace change, they have to see us walking the walk."

Karen spoke up. "And if some leaders aren't comfortable coaching?"

"Then we train them first," Sean replied. "A lot of people get promoted because they are good at the job—not because they know how to lead. We fix that by building their coaching skills, not just handing them metrics."

David asked, "So everyone's expected to coach?"

"Every single one," Sean said.

Marcus smirked. "That'll ruffle some feathers."

Sean grinned. "Maybe, but not in this room."

Maria leaned forward. "What else do we need to make this work?"

Sean wrote on the board:

3. Support Tools That Make Change Easier

"We don't just train people and hope they figure it out—we make the right way the easy way," he said. "Outside of work, that might mean a simpler scheduling tool for a volunteer group, a better rehearsal format for a debate team, or a checklist app that keeps a youth sports league organized. Here, that means we work with our teams to constantly look for better ways of working. Not to work faster, but to work smarter and more efficiently."

James nodded. "Like how we're replacing those clunky spreadsheets with live tracking in the warehouse?"

"Exactly," Sean said. "When the system helps you, you want to use it. When it slows you down, you fight it."

Bill shook his head. "Most organizations stop here; they invest in change but forget to make it usable."

Sean underlined the word **Optimize.** "Training. Coaching. Support. This isn't about pushing change—it's about removing obstacles so people can pull change into what they do every day."

The following week, Sean gathered a group for the first phase of training.

"We're not here to tick boxes," he said. "We're here to build habits." He explained the concept of coaching kata—short, structured conversations repeated often until they become second nature.

"Think of a political candidate preparing for a big debate," Sean said. "They don't just read talking points once; they rehearse opening statements, practice answering tough questions, get feedback, and then do it again. They keep refining until it's automatic—until they can respond clearly even under pressure. That's kata in action."

He turned to the whiteboard and wrote:

KATA = Practice → Habit → Culture

"It's not about having all the answers," he said. "It's about developing the habit of thinking, adjusting, and improving together."

Maria leaned forward. "So, by doing it every day, it stops being a project and just becomes part of who we are?"

Sean smiled. "Exactly. And when improvement becomes a habit, that's when real change happens."

Chapter 16: Complete Incremental Milestones *(FOCUS)*

Sean stood in the middle of the press department, arms crossed, watching the controlled chaos unfold. The rhythmic clank of metal, the steady hum of machinery, and the occasional hiss of compressed air filled the space.

Sean and his leadership team stood in front of a small whiteboard. "Big change is daunting," Sean began, "but small wins build momentum."

It was the same lesson he'd used when helping his son Timmy get ready for his first 5K run. Timmy had wanted to quit in the first week because three miles felt impossible. They started with small goals— just making it to the next mailbox, then the next block, then half a mile without stopping. Those small wins built confidence until the full distance didn't feel so overwhelming.

"First test?" Sean said to the group. "Reducing changeover times."

Applying the Coaching Kata

Sean walked over to Press #4 as Terry finished a changeover. "We're going to use the Coaching Kata for this," Sean said.

Maria crossed her arms, smiling. "Alright, walk us through it."

Sean wheeled over a portable whiteboard and wrote out the five Coaching Kata questions from the framework in Mike Rother's book, which he had gifted to each of his leaders a few weeks prior:

1. **What is the target condition?**

2. **What is the actual condition now?**

3. **What obstacles do you think are preventing you from reaching the target condition? Which one are you addressing now?**

4. **What is your next step (next experiment)? What do you expect?**

5. **How quickly can we go and see what we have learned from taking that step?**

He pointed at the press. "Let's start at the top. Bill?"

Bill pointed right back at the machine. "Target is a thirty-minute changeover."

"Actual?" Sean asked.

Maria checked her notes. "Last one was fifty-five minutes."

Sean looked at Terry. "What's getting in the way?"

Terry thought for a moment. "We waste time getting the new die in position—sometimes it's not ready. And alignment takes too long because every operator does it differently. No standardized settings."

Sean wrote on the board:

• **Dies not staged consistently before changeover**

• **Alignment varies by operator**

• **No standardized adjustment process**

"And which one are we tackling first?" Sean asked.

Bill replied, "Pre-staging the dies before the current job finishes."

Terry added, "And document alignment settings for each die type."

Sean circled both ideas. "Perfect, and how soon can we test this?"

Terry didn't hesitate. "Next changeover we'll see real numbers."

Coaching Bill to Coach Others

Sean turned to Bill. "You're going to coach your supervisors through this process."

Bill blinked. "Me?"

Sean grinned. "Yeah, you. You know this place better than anyone. Problem-solving must be a habit, not a one-off event."

"So, do I just ask these questions?" Bill asked.

"Exactly," Sean said. "But no giving them the answers—you guide them to find their own. Your job is to make them think, not to think for them."

Bill smirked. "Alright, I'll give it a shot."

Sean clapped him on the back. "Good. The faster we build this habit, the faster we stop getting problems reported and start getting problems solved."

Executing the Fixes

A few days later, the team gathered again. Dies were now pre-staged, saving fifteen minutes. Alignment was standardized—no more guessing. Bill had even run a quick micro-training to make sure everyone was on the same page.

Terry held a stopwatch. "Here we go."

• **Old die removed—10 minutes, down from 15**
• **New die inserted—5 minutes, down from 10**
• **Alignment—9 minutes, down from 20**
• **Final time: 29 minutes, 18 seconds**

Bill let out a loud, "Damn, that's the fastest I've seen it done."

Maria grinned. "And we're just getting started."

"One win down," Sean said.

Marcus patted him on the shoulder. "Let's stack 'em."

David added, "This is the fun part, gentlemen."

Sean thought back to his son's race. He didn't win, but he crossed the finish line smiling because he knew how far he had come. That was the thing about small wins; they not only moved you forward, but they also made you believe you could keep going. It was the same principle whether you were shaving minutes off a changeover, shedding five pounds at the gym, or finally paying down a stubborn credit card balance. Progress built confidence, and confidence created momentum.

Connecting Wins to Business

The next morning in the conference room, Marcus ran the numbers. "Before, we averaged fifty to sixty minutes per changeover. Now we're under thirty."

Sean nodded. "Impact on production?"

Marcus grinned. "Six changeovers per shift means we've gained three hours per shift—six hours per day. That's fifteen percent more output without adding labor or overtime."

David leaned forward. "What does that mean in terms of dollars?"

"If we sustain this across all presses," Marcus said, "about $500,000 in annual production capacity."

Karen added, "Also fewer late shipments, which helps our customer satisfaction scores."

Sean circled a note in his book: *Tie every improvement to business results—and to the human side of change.*

He looked up. "Let's share this with the team. They need to see that what they're doing isn't just faster; it's making us better, stronger, and more competitive."

Wins Beyond the Numbers

Sean paused, then added, "And remember, these improvements aren't just about hitting financial targets. They're about reducing stress on the floor. Think about it—no one enjoys being behind all day, scrambling to catch up. The same way no parent enjoys rushing every morning because the school bus is about to leave. Small fixes create breathing room, and breathing room gives people the capacity to do their best work."

Bill chuckled. "So, you're saying fewer late nights and fewer ulcers?"

"Exactly," Sean said with a grin. "And maybe a little less yelling at home because people aren't carrying the day's frustrations through the front door."

Maria leaned back in her chair. "The cool part is that people are starting to believe this is possible. They're not just going through the motions—they're actually leaning in."

"That's the secret," Sean said. "You don't need one big miracle. You need a steady drumbeat of progress. Just like training for a marathon— you don't start with twenty-six miles, you start with a single mile, then stack them week by week. Before long, what once seemed impossible becomes the new normal."

The group nodded. For the first time, the data on the board wasn't just a report—it was proof that the work mattered. Proof that effort wasn't wasted. Proof that change could stick.

Chapter 17: Utilizing Adequate Resources (FOCUS)

No amount of training or goal setting would matter if employees didn't have the resources to execute the changes. During a morning Gemba walk, Bill brought up an ongoing issue with one of the older press machines.

"This thing's a dinosaur," he said, tapping the side of the machine. "No matter how much we refine our process, we can't cut our changeover times if the machine itself is holding us back."

Sean had anticipated this. He had already been working with Jake Sr., the executive who had initially convinced him to take this role, to build a case for capital investment in new equipment.

After the morning walk of the floor, Sean went to his office, opened his laptop, and drafted an email to Jake Sr.

Subject: Time to Secure Equipment Investment

Jake,

The transformation is taking hold and real change is happening. The press team has successfully reduced changeover times and engagement is increasing across departments. We now have the data to prove that operational improvements are delivering measurable results:

- *Changeovers on Press #4 were reduced from 55 minutes to 29 minutes, adding six extra hours of production capacity per shift.*

- *First-pass quality on precision parts has increased from 82% to 94%, reducing rework and scrap costs by $20,000 per month.*

- *Inventory accuracy has improved from 76% to 98%, cutting down order fulfillment errors and reducing delays in shipping.*

- *Employees are driving continuous improvement—Bill's team in the press department initiated their own workflow adjustments, saving 15 minutes per cycle without additional cost.*

These improvements are making a real impact, but we're reaching the limits of what we can accomplish without upgrading key equipment. The team is working hard, but they're still battling inefficiencies caused by aging machines that can't keep up with demand.

- *Press #2 loses 15% efficiency per shift due to worn-out hydraulic systems, leading to frequent pressure fluctuations that slow production.*

- *The CNC lathe is running outdated software, requiring manual adjustments that add 20 minutes per setup, negating some of our recent process gains.*

- *One of our key finishing machines has an unrepairable motor issue, forcing us to reroute work and creating bottlenecks in final assembly.*

If we want to sustain this momentum and take our performance to the next level, we need to invest in the right tools. With updated presses, modernized CNC programming, and a reliable finishing system, we can:

✓ *Increase throughput by at least 12%, adding capacity without additional labor costs.*

✓ *Reduce scrap and rework by stabilizing machine precision, improving first-pass yield.*

✓ *Eliminate production bottlenecks that are delaying shipments and impacting customer satisfaction.*

It's time to deliver on new equipment. Now, before you say, "Sean, I already knew you were going to ask for money," let me remind you— you're the one who convinced me to leave the Army and step into this crazy world of turning companies around in the first place.

Mary still says I should have ignored you and opened a fishing charter instead. She claims my stress level would be lower, and I would still have my hair.

So, if nothing else, approve the equipment investment before she convinces me to quit and become a full-time boat captain. You and I both know I'd be terrible at it; I have zero patience for people who don't know how to bait a hook.

Looking forward to catching up (preferably about the investment, but I'll take a fishing trip too).

Best,
Sean

As he hit "send," Sean leaned back in his chair. Execution change wasn't just about starting strong; it was about sustaining momentum until the change became the new normal. Now, the real challenge lay ahead: scaling execution across the entire organization and securing the investments to sustain it.

Sustaining Accountability and Performance

A few weeks later, as Sean, his leadership team, and the change champions did their morning Gemba walk, Sean stopped and said the word many on the team had been thinking: *accountability.*

"This is where most transformations fall apart," Sean said. "The first few months have been exciting. People are engaged, and ideas are flowing. But at some point..."

"The reality sets in," Marcus finished.

To ensure the gains were sustained, they implemented daily performance reviews at the end of each shift, led by Bill and Maria. Operators were encouraged to report not only the numbers but also:

- What challenges they faced

- What improvements they suggested

This was creating a culture where employees weren't just following new processes, they were owning them.

Sean also made it clear that accountability applied to everyone, including leadership.

"If something isn't working, we fix it. If a process needs tweaking, we tweak it. But what we won't do is let things slide," Sean said.

"The novelty will wear off, challenges come up, and people slide back into old habits," he continued. "That's why we need a structure to hold ourselves accountable."

Marcus responded, "So, what does that structure look like?"

Sean ticked off the list with his fingers.

- Daily leadership huddles → Keep alignment tight.
- KPI tracking → No hiding from results.
- Monthly town halls → Check in on progress.
- Course correction → Fix the system before blaming people.

Marcus raised an eyebrow. "So, no room for excuses?"

"Nope," Sean said flatly. "But also, no room for finger-pointing. When performance dips, we fix the system and focus on the process rather than blaming individuals."

David exhaled. "Damn. This is going to be a ride."

Sean grinned. "That's why we're focusing. One step at a time, one win at a time."

"Alright, Sean, let's do this," Bill practically yelled from the back of the group.

With the foundation set, it was time to move forward—one step, one process, one win at a time.

Chapter 18: From One Win to Many

The following Monday, the leadership huddle felt different. Karen, usually reserved, spoke up first.

"I ran into Terry in the breakroom. He said—and I quote— 'It feels like we're finally fixing things instead of just talking about them.'"

Sean smiled. "That's exactly what we're going for. But here's the real test: how do we take this beyond the press department and customer service?"

David leaned forward. "The next biggest pain point is material flow. No matter how fast we change the presses or how quickly customer service resolves an issue, if material isn't staged properly, we're still losing time."

Marcus nodded. "Even with faster changeovers, we're still losing fifteen minutes a shift on average waiting for material."

Maria crossed her arms. "Then we bring the warehouse into this. If flow is the problem, let's fix that next."

Sean looked at James, the warehouse supervisor.

James rubbed his chin. "Honestly, our process is chaos. Forklifts crisscrossing like it's bumper cars at the county fair, material staged last minute, and half the time we don't know what's needed until someone yells for it."

Sean turned to the whiteboard and, in big block letters, wrote:

Next Focus: Material Flow → Zero Delays to the Presses

"Alright," Sean said, "what do we know?"

Karen flipped through her notes. "Material's getting staged too late."

Bill added, "Forklifts are fighting over space like it's the last parking spot at Costco on a Saturday."

James sighed. "We also don't have a real staging process. Everyone's winging it."

Sean underlined that last point. "That's the issue—we're reacting instead of preventing. Like waiting until your gas light's been on for two days and then being shocked when you're stranded on the side of the road."

The group chuckled.

"Before we jump to solutions," Sean continued, "go to the Gemba. Don't rely on secondhand stories; watch for yourself. Make sure you watch the process and ask questions of the subject matter experts, the ones who do it every day—before you hand out answers. Remember, curiosity is one of the most important traits of a good leader."

He turned to James. "I want you to lead this one. Map the process with your team—every step from inventory to press. Where's the waste? Where are the delays?"

James scribbled notes.

"Make sure we pull data," Sean added. "Pareto charts, time studies, smoke signals—I don't care how. Just bring the truth, not guesses."

Karen smiled. "The team will love seeing us use the same tools we trained them on."

"Exactly," Sean said. "This isn't a flavor-of-the-month fix—it's about building something better."

Driving Change Through Continuous Improvement

The next Monday, the leadership team and change champions gathered in the conference room. Butcher paper covered the wall, full of sticky notes, arrows, and hand-sketched process maps. James stood at the front of the room with two of his team leads.

He pointed to the left side, labeled *Current State.*

"We shadowed two full shifts. Talked to forklift drivers, operators, even maintenance. Here's what we found:

1. No visual cues for staging—people rely on last-minute texts or shouts.

2. Forklift congestion—like rush-hour traffic in a hallway.

3. No ownership of material readiness—everyone assumes someone else has it.

Then he gestured to the *Future State* side:

• **Color-coded staging zones for each press.**
• **Pre-shift readiness board.**
• **One-way traffic lanes to eliminate 'forklift chicken.'**
• **Five-minute kickoff huddles before shifts.**

Marcus nodded. "So, you're moving from 'just in case' to 'just in time.'"

James smiled. "Exactly."

Sean leaned forward. "You didn't just slap on a fix; you mapped, measured, and built it with the people doing the work. That's how change sticks."

Karen raised an eyebrow. "When do we start?"

James grinned. "We piloted it Friday and downtime dropped by sixty percent. Operators said it was the smoothest handoff they've seen."

Maria leaned back. "Let's roll it."

Sean smirked. "Careful, Maria. We're not turning this into a Southeastern Conference vs. Big Ten thing again with that Alabama Roll Tide talk."

Maria grinned ear to ear. "Roll Tide."

Sean groaned. "And that's why THE Ohio State University fans can't get along with you SEC folks."

The room burst into laughter, and Sean underlined two words on the board with a smile:

Ownership and Momentum

Chapter 19: Sustaining Accountability and Performance through KPIs (FOCU<u>S</u>)

As the changes took hold, Sean knew the hardest part wasn't getting people to try something new—it was keeping them from quietly sliding back into the old ways, like a dieter who swears off sugar... until they "accidentally" end up in the drive-thru for a milkshake. With execution in full swing, it was time to reinforce the last part of FOCUS—Sustaining Accountability and Performance.

They had learned that setting a vision and getting buy-in was one thing. Making change stick meant they had to:

- **Track progress relentlessly**
- **Hold each other accountable**
- **Keep momentum alive when the excitement faded**

Monitoring KPIs and Performance Metrics

The Obeya room buzzed with quiet energy as the leadership team and change champions gathered. Under each of the main headings that the team had already agreed would be the biggest levers, space had been left open for the KPIs that would bring those big words to life. This wasn't theory, it was where the team would decide what to measure, how to track it, and ultimately how to hold themselves accountable.

Sean stood in the middle of the room, marker in hand. "Alright, we've talked about why this matters, now we're going to decide what goes on the wall. If it doesn't tie to one of these six high-level measures, it doesn't get our attention right now."

He continued, "Think of it like keeping score in sports. You don't just say, 'We think we scored more points than them.' You write it down, you track it, and you make sure everyone knows the score. If it matters, it's visible."

Bill smirked. "Guess that means we can't keep running on excuses anymore."

Sean grinned. "Exactly, and the beauty of this system is that it's visual. Anyone can walk into this room, look at the wall, and know exactly how we're doing and what's being worked on."

Choosing the Right Metrics

Marcus stepped forward with a handful of notes. "Alright, let's start simple. Under Engagement, we track Employee Satisfaction, Turnover Rates, and Idea Generation. Those tell us whether people are leaning in or checking out."

Karen added, "Under Quality, we measure Defect Rates and Customer Complaints. If those numbers don't move, nothing else matters."

"Delivery's easy," James said. "On-time Shipments and Schedule Adherence."

Maria chimed in from the back. "Don't forget Safety—Incident Rates and Near Misses. If people aren't safe, none of the rest counts."

Sean nodded. "Perfect, and here's the key: these KPIs aren't leadership's numbers—they're the company's. They're visible to everyone, and they're owned by the people closest to the work."

Making It Real

David leaned against the wall. "What happens if the numbers don't look good? What if engagement dips or defect rates spike?"

Sean pointed to the wall. "Then we know where to focus. It's not about blaming, it's about learning. Every dip is a signal that tells us where to coach, where to experiment, and where to improve. The Obeya is our scoreboard."

Maria chimed in, "Sounds great, but what if these numbers fade faster than a New Year's resolution?"

Sean wrote across the Engagement wall in big letters:

Accountability = Ownership + Follow-Through

"We don't manage this monthly," he said. "That's like checking your bank account every quarter—you're broke before you even know it. Accountability happens daily; in huddles, in coaching conversations, and right here, on this wall."

Chapter 20: Execution Pays Off – The Equipment Investment

It started with a low rumble, followed by the distinct hiss of brakes coming to a stop. Out in the loading bay, a massive flatbed truck pulled up, carrying crates of brand-new press equipment.

Sean stood near the dock, watching as the forklift operators began unloading. Around him, several employees had stopped to take in the sight.

Bill was the first to say anything. "I'll be damned."

Maria smiled. "Guess he wasn't bluffing."

James, standing beside them, exhaled. "I don't think we've had new machines since before I got here."

Sean turned to them, a grin spreading across his face. "If we'd asked for this six months ago, do you think we would have gotten it?"

Bill shook his head. "Not a chance."

Laying Groundwork Before the Investment

Later that morning, Sean gathered the leadership team and change champions around one of the newly uncrated machines.

"This right here," he said, placing a hand on the sleek metal surface, "is why we spent months doing the groundwork first. If we had just bought new equipment without fixing our processes, training our teams, and building accountability, this would've been just another expensive Band-Aid."

Marcus nodded. "If we'd made this investment without proving we could sustain improvements, it would've been wasted money."

"Exactly," Sean continued. "The FOCUS model wasn't just about process change; it was about making sure we could sustain and maximize investments like this. Think about it like remodeling your kitchen—if you don't fix the leaky roof first, you're going to have a really nice kitchen for a short period of time until that leaking roof ruins everything."

He turned to Bill. "You're the most experienced guy in this department. What do you think would have happened if we had dropped this here without the last several months of work?"

Bill ran his hand over his chin. "It would've been a disaster. People wouldn't have known how to use it properly, maintenance wouldn't have been set up, and we'd still be fighting the same old problems—just with shinier equipment."

Sean clapped him on the back. "That's the key—technology is an enabler, not a solution. Same way a treadmill won't make you fit if you never step on it."

Karen crossed her arms, smiling. "You mean treadmills aren't to hang dirty clothes on, like my husband thinks?"

Sean smiled and looked at Bill. "Works for me. How about you, Bill?"

"I don't see a problem with that," he said as the group laughed.
From Change to Culture – The Shift Takes Hold

Within a week, the first of the new presses was fully installed. Operators had gone through structured hands-on training, guided by coaching kata routines—daily, focused conversations between team leads and frontline employees that helped embed the new standards into their day-to-day rhythm.

Rather than dumping information in a one-time workshop, learning was now happening where the work happened, in small, practical steps. It was becoming habit. The early results were impossible to ignore. The first trial runs had already cut changeover times even further, smashing the thirty-minute goal Sean and Bill had set months ago. More importantly, the improvement wasn't being driven by outside pressure—it was coming from within.

Walking around the production floor, Sean could feel it. The resistance—the crossed arms, the guarded expressions, the "I've seen this before" shrugs—was gone. In its place was something very different: quiet momentum.

Maria caught him near the press line and motioned toward a group of operators clustered around a whiteboard, mid-discussion.

"You're seeing this, right?"

Sean raised an eyebrow. "Seeing what?"

She pointed toward the operators who were debating a minor tweak to their changeover sequence. No supervisor was prompting them, and no checklist was driving it. They were doing it because they wanted to.

"This," she said. "People figuring out how to make things better on their own."

Sean smiled. "That's the difference between compliance and commitment. It's the same thing you see when your kids clean their room without being told—rare, but glorious when it happens."

Bill, walking past with a clipboard, overheard and gave Sean a light punch on the arm. "Alright, don't get all 'leadership guru' on us again. But... you were right, this feels different."

James, who'd led the earlier material flow improvements, nodded from across the floor. "We're finally not just reacting; we're ahead for once."

Sean just took it in—watching as one of the team leads coached a new hire through the pre-shift checklist, while another group updated their hourly visual management board without being asked. The boards weren't flashy, but they were theirs. The team had reworked them three times in the last week—evidence of ownership, not obligation. The boards were also covered in leaders' initials, including his, showing employees that what they were doing mattered while also building accountability.

Embedding the New Normal

Sean knew better than to celebrate too soon. Results were great, but sustainability was the true test of culture. Anyone could launch a change initiative; the real question was: would it last?

At the next weekly meeting, the team walked through the numbers on the Obeya, but no one really needed to look at the metrics to tell them what they were already feeling on the floor.

126

Marcus ran through the numbers. "Turnover has dipped considerably, and employee participation in problem-solving has more than doubled. Customer satisfaction is tracking up for the third week straight."

David leaned forward. "That's good, but what about the biggest indicator?"

Sean smiled. "The biggest indicator isn't on this wall."

He paused, letting the weight of the moment land.

"It's on the floor and in the conversations. The way operators are leading huddles, asking better questions, suggesting improvements. People aren't just doing what they're told; they're driving the change themselves. It's like a good habit at home—once you don't have to remind someone to put the milk back in the fridge, you know you've made progress."

Tom smiled. "I never thought I'd say this, but… it actually feels like we're running a company instead of just surviving day to day."

Karen grinned. "We should put that on a t-shirt."

The room laughed, but it was the kind of laugh that comes with pride, not relief.

This wasn't the kind of change that fizzled after the consultants left or the boss got bored. It was different. This change was woven into the daily fabric of how the company operated. Change wasn't being pushed anymore, it was being pulled from the ground up.

Sean looked around the room. Some of these leaders had resisted him at first, while others had been cautiously optimistic. But now, they were united—not by mandates, but by mission.

"This isn't the end of execution," Sean said. "It's the beginning of a new way of working. Now, our job is to protect it, coach it, and keep evolving it—always thinking about better ways of working."

He paused, then added quietly, "Because culture doesn't live in the strategy, it lives in the behaviors we tolerate and the ones we reinforce."

With that, the transformation wasn't just something they were doing, it was something they had become. Summit Manufacturing had started the climb, and this time, they weren't coming back down.

Chapter 21: The Ripple Effect

Customer Service and then the Press Department had been the proving ground. Changeovers were faster, downtime had dropped, and employees, once skeptical, now believed in the process. But that was only the beginning. Across the plant, the ripple effects of the change were becoming harder to ignore.

In shipping, James and his team had redesigned their staging process, cutting delays and congestion in half. In the warehouse, the team had rolled out a visual management system that was already helping identify inventory mismatches before they became emergencies. Even in support departments like planning and scheduling, people were beginning to apply what they had learned in the continuous improvement sessions—mapping out processes, reviewing data, and challenging assumptions that had gone unquestioned for years.

The customer service and press department might have been the spark, but the fire was spreading, and not because leadership had forced it. Sean and his team had managed something most organizations never get right: they had created pull, not push. No one had plastered slogans in the breakroom or rolled out an "everyone must comply by Friday" mandate. Instead, they focused on one area, proved it worked, and let curiosity do the rest.

Sean stood in the middle of the factory floor, arms folded, watching Maria lead a small group from the assembly area through a walk-and-talk. She pointed toward the press line, where Bill and his team had just completed another sub-thirty-minute changeover with calm precision.

"This is what we've been working toward," Maria said. "Before any of you say, 'That works in your area, but not ours,' let me remind you—Bill said the exact same thing."

Bill, overhearing, grinned. "Yep, and I was wrong. Mark this day on your calendars, folks, because it doesn't happen often."

A few chuckles broke out.

Sean jumped in. "This isn't about copying every step they took. It's about adopting the same approach—go to where the work happens, map out the process, involve your team, and fix what you can control."

Alex, one of the assembly workers, crossed his arms. "Yeah, but press is different from assembly. You have machines running most of the time. We're dealing with people, assembly lines, hand tools, shifting demand. How's that supposed to work here?"

Sean smiled. "Fair point, but think about it like organizing your kitchen. You don't remodel the whole house; you fix the one drawer you open fifty times a day, so it's not jammed with spatulas, batteries, and that one random Allen wrench."

Maria laughed. "You do have a weirdly specific example ready to go."

Sean smirked. "Maria, I bet you'd write 'Go Tide' on a whiteboard at home if you could spell it."

The group laughed and Bill jumped in. "Careful, Sean—you keep that up and she's gonna put your name under 'waste' on the board."

Sean shot back, "At least I'd be in good company—Bill's been holding the title for years."

Bill grinned, shaking his head. "Touché."

Back to business, Sean turned to James. "So, what's the most frustrating inefficiency in the warehouse right now?"

"Order picking," James said without hesitation. "Too much back and forth, lost inventory, and missed shipments. The team has been begging for us to work with them to help fix it."

"Then that's where we go next," Sean said. "Just like in press, we break it down. Work with your team to find the biggest cause of lost time."

Maria smirked. "You're not gonna like the answer, Sean—we already know."

James sighed. "Paper-based tracking."

Karen frowned. "And what's stopping us from upgrading?"

Marcus, the CFO, shrugged. "Money. It always comes back to money."

Sean nodded. "Then we prove the return just like we did in the press department. We'll start small, track the wasted time, and show the case for change. Once we prove it works here, the next department will want in—not because we forced them, but because they saw it work."

Seeing the Change Firsthand

Later that afternoon, Sean walked with James through the warehouse, clipboard in hand. The space was buzzing with movement—forklifts beeping, workers navigating tight aisles, boxes being loaded onto pallets. At first glance, it looked like a well-oiled machine, but Sean had learned to see beyond the motion.

"Watch this," James said, gesturing toward a worker at the far end of the aisle. The man flipped through a handwritten pick list, scanning shelves for a part number. A few moments passed before he shook his head and disappeared around the corner.

"See that?" James said. "He can't find the item, so now he's walking back to the supervisor to ask where it is."

Sean checked his watch. "And how often does that happen?"

"Too often," James replied. "Add it up, and we lose hours each week just on searching for inventory."

They moved further down the aisle where another worker, Lisa, had just found what she was looking for. She jotted something down on her pick list and walked toward a loading dock.

Sean stopped her. "Hey Lisa, mind if I ask you how you track what you just pulled?"

Lisa held up her clipboard. "We mark it here, then hand it off at the end of the shift for someone to update the system."

Sean glanced at James, who gave him a knowing smile.

"So, if something gets misplaced between now and when it's entered?" Sean asked.

Lisa shrugged. "Then we go hunting for it, or someone pulls the wrong item tomorrow."

Sean sighed. This was waste in plain sight, and it wasn't just about inefficiency; it was about frustration, lost time, and human error compounding over time.

As they walked off the floor, Sean turned to James. "You ready to shake things up some more?"

James grinned. "Been waiting for you to say that."

Chapter 22: Sustaining the Gains – Making Change Stick

Sean walked into the conference room where the leadership team had gathered for their monthly review. The mood was different than it had been just a few months ago. People weren't just waiting to hear another presentation; they were engaged. They wanted to see the numbers, discuss progress, and find ways to keep pushing forward.

Marcus had the KPI dashboard displayed on the projector. The numbers told a clear story:

- Press department changeover times reduced by 42%
- Warehouse picking accuracy improved by 20%
- Employee engagement—idea submissions tripled since the beginning of the initiative
- Turnover rates were holding steady, with early indications of a downward trend

Sean leaned against the table, a grin on his face. "Not a bad start."

Karen smiled. "I have to admit, I didn't expect to see this kind of improvement this soon."

James nodded. "The biggest difference is that people actually believe it now. Before, they thought this was just another 'flavor-of-the-month' initiative, but they see things changing and sticking."

The Challenge of Sustaining Success

Bill, who had been unusually quiet, finally spoke up. "So, what stops us from backsliding?"

It was the question everyone was thinking but hadn't asked yet.

Sean stepped forward. "Great question, Bill. This is the part where a lot of change efforts go wrong. It's like getting in shape, you can drop twenty pounds for a wedding or vacation because you've got a short-term goal. But when the trip or honeymoon is over, if you don't keep the same habits, the weight comes right back. The same is true for any big change. Starting is exciting, but the grind of keeping it going is where most people and organizations stumble."

Maria smirked. "Oh good, I was worried we were going to get complacent."

Sean chuckled. "Not a chance. Here's the deal: winning is easy, sustaining is hard. It's like training for a marathon—the race is only one day. The real challenge is putting in the miles, rain or shine, day after day leading up to the race. This dashboard," he said, tapping the KPI screen, "doesn't mean we're done. It means we've proven we can change. Now we make sure we don't lose ground."

He turned to Marcus. "What do we need to keep tracking to make sure we don't slip?"

Marcus gestured at the screen. "Turnover is still our biggest unknown. Engagement is high now, but we need to see if it translates to long-term retention. It's critical that we track process adherence; just because we trained people doesn't mean they'll keep following the new way."

Sean nodded. "Sounds about right. So how do we stay accountable, team?"

Bill leaned against the table. "That's the real challenge. I've seen it before—new process works great for a few weeks, then people start sliding back into old habits. Like someone who organizes their garage and swears they'll keep it that way, but three months later you can't even see the workbench."

Sean grinned. "Which is why we need Standard Work."

Maria raised an eyebrow. "Standard Work?"

Sean turned to the board. **How We Stay Accountable**

- **Standard Work: Every process has a best-known method**
- **Audits: We verify that Standard Work is being followed**
- **Feedback Loop: If a better way is found, we update the Standard Work**
- **Visibility: KPIs track whether process adherence leads to sustained results**

"It's how we make sure improvements stick," Sean explained. "We document the best way to do the job—the most efficient, safest, highest-quality way. Then we train to it, follow it, and update it when the people doing the work find a better way. That's how you keep the garage clean, so to speak."

Marcus nodded slowly. "So instead of hoping people stick with the new process, we define it, track it, and reinforce it?"

"Exactly," Sean said.

Bill nodded. "If people stop following the process, it's either because they weren't trained well or they found a better way. Either way, we need to know."

"Exactly," Sean replied. "Also keep in mind that people doing the job are the experts. We build the Standard Work with them, and we don't just 'invite' them to improve it—we expect them to."

Dave grinned. "So, we define and document a best way to do each process with the true subject matter experts, and we make continuous improvement part of the job description."

"Exactly," Sean said.

Karen folded her arms. "I hate to be the voice of doom, but let's be real. People are excited now, but what happens when things go wrong?"

James sighed. "She's right. Eventually, something will break down, or we'll hit a wall, and old habits will try to creep back in."

"Which is why," Sean said, "we need a playbook for when things start slipping." He wrote on the board:

The 'Oh Crap' Plan

1. **Spot the slippage early—KPIs, feedback loops, and leadership visibility must stay strong**
2. **Reinforce the why—remind people why they changed in the first place**
3. **Coach, don't blame—if teams start slipping, retrain and support instead of punishing**

4. Celebrate small wins—acknowledge when teams catch and fix issues early

Bill scratched his head. "So… when things start to suck, we don't just yell at people?"

Accountability Without Fear: The Lesson from the Night Shift

Sean smiled, shaking his head. "No, Bill. If we start blaming people for backsliding, they'll hide problems instead of fixing them."

Bill raised an eyebrow. "You really think people would go that far to cover up mistakes?"

Sean leaned back, crossing his arms. "Let me tell you a story about a company I worked with years ago. We had a major issue with quality defects—things slipping through that should have been caught. Leadership decided to start tracking quality performance by shift. A few weeks in, the night shift had perfect quality numbers—100% every night."

James shook his head. "That's never a good sign."

Sean nodded. "Exactly. I knew something wasn't right because not many operations run at 100% quality without fail. There are always issues—small mistakes, machine hiccups, human errors. But this report said zero defects for months. So, I grabbed the night shift manager, and we decided to go to the gemba—to the floor, at two in the morning, to see for ourselves."

Maria raised an eyebrow. "Let me guess, it wasn't exactly what you expected?"

Sean chuckled. "Not even close. We walked in, and at first, everything looked normal. The machines were running, operators were at their stations, and the quality inspection system was up. But then, as we got closer to the inspection station, we saw something that made us stop dead in our tracks."

Karen leaned in. "What was it?"

Sean grinned. "A broom handle was jammed against the 'start' button on the quality scanner."

Silence.

Then Maria burst out laughing. "Wait—you're telling me someone rigged the machine to skip quality checks?"

Sean nodded. "Yup. The scanner that was supposed to flag defects was completely disabled. The machine just kept processing parts as if every single one was perfect."

Bill shook his head in disbelief. "And no one noticed?"

"Oh, the shift supervisor noticed," Sean said. "He let it happen. He knew if the quality numbers were bad, his boss would tear him apart, maybe even fire him. So, he told his guys, 'Just keep the numbers clean,' and one of the younger employees took that literally."

James sighed. "So instead of fixing quality, they just hid it."

Sean nodded. "Exactly, and that's what happens in a blame culture. People don't solve problems; they hide them. They game the system and make sure they don't get in trouble instead of making sure things actually improve."

Maria leaned back, shaking her head. "Damn. So, what happened?"

"We shut down production that night and fixed the issue immediately. But more importantly, we didn't punish the guy who wedged the broom in there. We changed the way leadership handled accountability. Instead of demanding perfect numbers, we asked supervisors to report what was really happening. We rewarded teams for catching and fixing problems, not for making things look flawless on paper."

Sean glanced around the table. "Here's the kicker: real quality improved overnight. Not because we got stricter, but because people stopped hiding the truth."

Bill shook his head. "That's wild."

James added, "Makes sense, though. If people are afraid of getting blamed, they'll do whatever it takes to avoid looking bad."

"Exactly," Sean said. "So, when we talk about sustaining accountability, it's not just about tracking numbers. It's about creating an environment where people can be honest about when things go wrong. Because they will go wrong, and they need to trust that leadership will help them fix it instead of just looking for someone to blame."

Karen nodded slowly. "So, in other words, no broomsticks on the start button."

Maria smirked. "Unless, of course, we're trying to hit some record-breaking efficiency metrics."

Sean groaned. "You know what, forget I told you that story."

The room erupted in laughter, but the message had landed. Accountability had to be about learning and fixing problems, not fear and punishment.

Maria leaned forward. "And what about leadership? What if you guys start slipping?"

Sean grinned. "Glad you asked. Accountability isn't just for the frontline—it's for us, too."

Karen raised an eyebrow. "So, we get to call you out?"

Sean laughed. "You get to coach us, just as we would do with you. No yelling."

James nudged Maria. "I think he just gave us permission to be annoying."

Maria smirked. "Oh, I was going to be annoying regardless."

Sean shook his head with a chuckle. "Here's the deal: accountability goes both ways. If we're not keeping up our end, you tell us. That's how we sustain this long-term."

The transformation had taken hold. Now, the challenge was making sure it lasted.

Chapter 23: Ongoing Training – Keeping the Momentum Alive

Sean stood in front of a packed training room. Employees from multiple departments sat together, flipping through training materials. Some looked engaged while others looked like they'd rather be at the dentist.

Sean raised an eyebrow. "Alright, let's start with the obvious question. Who here hates training?"

A few hands shot up.

Maria, sitting near the back, grinned. "Be honest, people. If you could skip this, would you?"

More hands went up.

Sean laughed. "Good, at least you're honest. I've been in trainings where I wanted to fake a phone call from my kid's school just to get out of it."

He clicked to the first slide:

Why Typical Training Sucks:

1. **It's boring.**
2. **It's disconnected from reality.**
3. **It's a waste of time.**

"Sound about right?" he asked.

A few people nodded, and one even said "Amen" under their breath.

Sean smirked. "Then let's not do that. Think of this like learning to ride a bike. You don't start with a three-hour PowerPoint on bicycle safety; you start by wobbling down the driveway with someone jogging next to you. Same thing here."

He turned to James. "What's the biggest issue in the warehouse right now?"

James exhaled. "Guys are still getting used to the new picking system. Some are hesitant, they're worried it's going to slow them down."

Sean pointed at him. "That's exactly why we're doing daily micro-trainings. Five to fifteen minutes, every shift, using real examples. Like how a basketball team practices inbound plays over and over, not a six-hour lecture on the history of basketball."

Bill raised an eyebrow. "So, no corporate slideshow nonsense?"

"None," Sean confirmed. "Training must be real-world, fast, and practical. If it doesn't help you today, it's useless—like learning advanced calculus to figure out a restaurant tip."

Leaders Leading from the Floor

Sean clicked to the next slide: **Leaders Engage**.

"I'm gonna say this loud and clear: training is not just for hourly associates; it's also for leaders."

Karen raised an eyebrow. "How do we make sure leaders actually show up?"

Sean grinned. "Simple, we track it. If you're in a leadership role, you need to be out there coaching and reinforcing, not leading from your office like some kind of remote-control manager."

Maria smirked. "So, I have permission to drag people onto the floor?"

Sean fired back. "Wait, are you actually asking for permission to do something? Did you hit your head this morning?"

The room erupted in laughter.

Embedding Accountability into Training

Sean moved to the whiteboard and wrote:

1. Train daily

2. Reinforce on the floor

3. Recognize improvement immediately

"If we don't do these three things, this whole transformation falls apart. It's not just about learning, it's about habit-building. It's like brushing your teeth—doing it once a month isn't going to cut it. You've gotta do it consistently, or the decay sets in."

James leaned forward. "So, what happens if people still resist?"

Sean's expression hardened. "Then we listen and find out why. Maybe it's frustration, or maybe it's fear—like a kid refusing to jump off the diving board because they think the water's cold. But if someone is just flat-out refusing to adapt, then we make it clear this is the new way forward."

He paused, then smiled. "If they still don't like it, we can always hand them a three-hour PowerPoint on the history of bicycle safety as punishment."

The room laughed again, but they also got the point. Training wasn't about filling seats, it was about building skills, confidence, and ownership.

Chapter 24: Securing the Warehouse Management System

Sean had been waiting for this email. Sitting at his desk, he refreshed his inbox, tapping his fingers on the wood. The subject line popped up: **Funding Approved – Now Stop Begging** from Jake Sr.

Sean clicked it open, scanning quickly before exhaling with a grin.

They had done it.

He leaned back, stretching, feeling the tension he'd been carrying for weeks begin to release. This wasn't just another win; it was validation that their process was working. The press department had exceeded expectations, and now, the next domino was falling.

His phone buzzed. It was Jake Sr.

"Well," Jake's voice came through before Sean could even say hello, "I'm impressed—but don't let it go to your head."

Sean smiled. "Oh, believe me, I won't. You made sure I had to justify this thing six different ways before you pulled the trigger."

Jake chuckled. "Damn right I did. I wasn't about to throw a pile of money at a warehouse management system just because you gave me a nice PowerPoint."

"PowerPoint?" Sean scoffed. "Jake, I literally dragged you down here, walked you through the process, and made you listen to Bill rant about inefficiencies for three hours."

"I almost didn't survive that," Jake replied.

Sean grinned. "But you signed off."

Jake sighed. "Yeah, because the numbers don't lie. The press department is saving hundreds of hours monthly, quality's up, and for the first time in a decade people are excited about the future of Summit." He paused. "So yeah, I'm on board. But you have ninety days to prove this investment was worth it. Otherwise, I'll make sure your next PowerPoint is about why we're shutting it down."

Sean groaned. "You have such a way with motivation."

Jake chuckled. "That's why you love me."

"I tolerate you," Sean corrected.

"Keep telling yourself that," Jake shot back before hanging up.

Sean set his phone down, still grinning.

He pulled out his notebook, jotted a few notes, then called Maria and James into his office.

They walked in, Maria looking mildly suspicious. "Please tell me you didn't call us here to ask about the coffee machine again."

Sean smiled. "Better—we got the funding."

James' eyes widened. "For the warehouse management system?"

Sean nodded.

Maria couldn't hold back her excitement. "Damn, I thought Jake was going to make us suffer a little longer."

"Oh, he did," Sean said. "But we sold it. Now, the real work begins."

He pulled up the rollout plan on his laptop.

"Phase one: We start small. One picking zone, five employees. We train them, test the system, prove it works, and when it does, we scale."

James nodded. "And if it doesn't work?"

Sean grinned. "Then we learn, adjust, and move forward."

Chapter 25: Implementing the System

Monday morning, the warehouse buzzed with nervous energy. The first five employees chosen for the warehouse management system pilot gathered around James, who was holding a tablet loaded with the software.

Sean stood nearby, watching.

"Alright," James started. "Who here has ever lost a pick sheet?"

A few hands went up.

Maria raised an eyebrow. "Only a few of you? Come on, be honest."

Every hand went up.

James smirked. "Yeah, that's what I thought. Well, today, we start fixing that." He held up the tablet. "No more paper lists and no more missing orders. This system will tell you exactly what to pick, where to go, and whether you pulled the right thing."

Luis, a veteran employee, folded his arms. "So, a robot's gonna tell me how to do my job now?"

Sean stepped in. "No, Luis. It's a tool to make your job easier. But if you want, I can personally follow you around and tell you how to do your job instead."

Luis smirked. "Hard pass, boss."

Karen, standing at the back, chimed in. "Look, we know change is frustrating. But remember what happened in press? At first, everyone pushed back. Now, they'd fight anyone who tried to take their improvements away."

James nodded. "Same thing here, all we ask is that you give it a fair shot. If it sucks, tell us why; but don't just write it off because it's new."

Luis sighed. "Okay, let's do it."

The First Week: Wins and Frustrations

By Friday, the early data was promising:

- Picking accuracy improved by 15%.
- Time spent looking for misplaced items decreased significantly.
- User adoption was mixed.

Some employees embraced the system immediately, while others were skeptical and frustrated by the learning curve.

Maria stood with Bill, watching from a distance. "You ever notice how people say they want things to be easier, but then complain when you change things?"

Bill chuckled. "Yeah, change sounds great until it happens to you."

Breaking Through with Resilience

Three weeks in, progress was undeniable:

- Picking times improved by 22%.
- Errors dropped by nearly 30%.
- Adoption was climbing—but not fast enough.

Sean walked into the warehouse and found Luis standing by the racks, a confused look on his face.

Sean stopped next to him. "Something on your mind?"

Luis sighed. "Okay, I'll admit it, this thing works better than I thought. But it's still tough for some of the guys because not everyone is great with technology."

Sean nodded. "So, what do you think we should do about it?"

Luis hesitated, then scratched his beard. "Some of the older guys could use more hands-on help, I don't know, maybe a buddy system? Pair them with someone who's picked it up faster?"

Sean grinned. "See, Luis, that's leadership. You just built our next training plan."

Luis rolled his eyes. "Yeah, yeah, just don't make me teach a class."

Sean clapped him on the shoulder. "Sorry, Luis, I can't promise you that."

Scaling for the Future

Sean leaned against the railing, looking down at the shop floor from above. It was different now, more energy, a lot of momentum and ownership.

Bill stepped up beside him. "Place looks good."

Sean nodded. "Yeah, it does."

Bill exhaled. "I ain't gonna lie, boss, when you showed up, I thought it was just another corporate shake-up. Another flavor of the month."

Sean smiled. "And now?"

Bill chuckled. "Now I get it." He shook his head. "It ain't about fixing one thing, it's about never stopping—making one improvement at a time and constantly evaluating, executing, and sustaining."

Sean smiled. Bill had come full circle.

Sean turned to him. "I don't want to sound cheesy, Bill, but I want you to know how proud I am of you."

Bill smiled. "We aren't going to hug it out, are we, boss?"

"No," Sean replied. "But I am promoting you to Shift Manager."

Bill blinked. "Wait—what?"

"You've been leading beyond just the press department," Sean said. "People listen to you, and you've been coaching operators in assembly, helping with logistics, stepping in wherever you're needed. You're already running the shift; you just don't have the title."

Bill rubbed his jaw, processing. "I dunno Sean. I'm a shop guy; do you really think I should be managing the whole shift?"

Sean smiled. "Bill, you've already been doing it."

Bill let out a slow breath. "Damn," he said as he shook his head. "Never thought I'd move up like this."

Sean clapped him on the back. "You earned it, Bill. Not because of how long you've been here, but because you're making this place better—and that's leadership."

Bill exhaled, then finally nodded. "Alright, let's do it."

Sean smiled. This was real change—not just fixing a company, but helping people step into something bigger than they ever expected.

At the next leadership meeting, Marcus walked through the latest warehouse KPIs:

- Error rates: Down 27%.
- Efficiency: Up 20%.
- Adoption rate: Steadily climbing.

Marcus leaned back. "We're getting close to proving the full ROI."

Karen smirked. "Which means Jake will finally shut up."

Sean chuckled. "For about five minutes before he asks what's next."

Bill folded his arms. "So, what is next?"

Sean exhaled. "We do what we said we'd do: repeat the process."

Karen tapped her fingers on the table. "Which department?"

Sean grinned. "Let's see who wants it."

Chapter 26: The Last Call

It was two months later, and Sean stood on the second-floor catwalk overlooking the production floor. Below him, machines hummed, operators moved with purpose, and the energy in the building was unrecognizable from the day he first walked in.

Back then, Summit Manufacturing had been on the edge of crisis. A company weighed down by inefficiency, a workforce resigned to the status quo, and a leadership team unsure of how to turn things around. Change had been needed, but no one truly believed it could happen.

Now, things were much different.

- Safety: Recordable incidents were down 40%. Near-miss reporting was up, showing people weren't hiding problems anymore—they were surfacing them.
- Quality: First-pass yield had climbed to 96%, cutting rework and scrap costs significantly.
- Delivery: On-time delivery jumped from 78% to 95%, winning back clients who had nearly walked away.
- Cost/Productivity: Changeover times were down 50%, unlocking thousands of additional production hours per year.
- Engagement: Turnover was down, idea submissions had doubled, and employee-led improvements filled entire walls of A3s.

Yet Sean knew real success wasn't in the numbers, it was in the mindset shift. He glanced across the floor to see Bill, now a Shift

Manager, running an improvement huddle with his team. He remembered how Bill had once been one of the biggest skeptics. Now, he was leading the charge, coaching others, and proving that change wasn't something that happened to you; it was something you built as a team. Sean smiled. This was real change.

Behind him, Marcus approached. "So," he said, leaning on the railing, "we've come a long way."

Sean nodded. "Yeah, we have."

"Are you staying?" Marcus asked. "Or are you off to your next project?"

Sean exhaled, looking down at the floor one more time. He had spent his career fixing broken things: companies, teams, systems—even himself. It was what he did.

But this, this was different. This wasn't just a turnaround; it was a foundation. Summit Manufacturing wasn't just better than it had been, it was now capable of sustaining its success, of continuously improving, and of thriving without him.

And that meant his job was done.

Sean turned to Marcus. "This team's got it from here."

Marcus smiled. "Didn't think I'd say this when you first showed up, but... we're gonna miss you."

Sean raised an eyebrow. "That almost sounded sincere. Are you feeling okay?"

Marcus rolled his eyes. "Fine, don't get all sentimental about it."

Sean grinned. "Just don't screw it up."

Marcus clapped him on the back. "No promises, but if we do, I'll wait a respectful three months before calling you to come fix it."

Sean laughed. "Make it six."

Marcus smirked. "We both know you'd be bored by then."

Sean took one last look at the floor, then turned toward the exit. He'd barely made it halfway when he heard Marcus's voice behind him.

"Hey—hold up a sec, there's something we need you for in the Obeya room."

Sean frowned. "Marcus, you know I'm not really big on goodbyes. I'm trying to make a clean exit here."

Marcus smirked. "Yeah, well, too bad. You're not done until we say you're done."

Against his better judgment, Sean followed him down the hall. As they rounded the corner, he saw the door to the Obeya room closed. Marcus swung it open.

Inside, the entire leadership team was gathered, along with all the change champions—Maria, Bill, Karen, James, David—and half the plant floor crew. They were standing around a giant, freshly cleaned whiteboard. Someone had decorated it with markers and sticky notes in every color imaginable. Above the board, a hastily hung sign read:

The Sean Memorial Whiteboard & Celsius Storage Facility

Sean stopped in his tracks, grinning. "Memorial? You make it sound like I'm dead."

Maria crossed her arms with a smirk. "Well, we figured this was the only way you'd stop trying to 'improve' our handwriting on the boards."

Bill chimed in. "We were gonna call it 'The Shrine of Endless Markers,' but that sounded creepy."

Karen handed him a marker. "Your turn, boss. Sign it before we auction it off on eBay."

Sean stepped forward, shaking his head. "You people are ridiculous." He uncapped the marker and scrawled in big block letters: **Keep Improving—or I'll Come Back.**

The room erupted in laughter.

Marcus raised his hand for silence. "Seriously, Sean—thank you. Not just for everything you did for the company, but for reminding us that leadership is about doing things with people, not to them. We're gonna keep this going."

Sean's grin softened. "I know you will. That's why I can leave without worrying. And I hope you know I love all of you and am so proud of what we have accomplished."

Maria, with a tear in her eye asked, "So are you heading straight home now?"

Sean nodded. "Yeah, time to trade in whiteboards for a weekend on the boat."

As he turned to go, the whole team called out in unison, "Don't forget your markers!"

As he walked toward the exit, Sean took one last look at the floor, then walked outside. He pulled out his phone and dialed.

After two rings, Mary answered. "Hey, stranger. Are you heading home yet?"

Sean smiled, his shoulders relaxing for the first time in months. "Yes ma'am, job's done. I'll be home by dinner."

Mary chuckled. "Good, because if you weren't, I was gonna start looking up fishing charter licenses for you."

Sean laughed, shaking his head. "Not happening, but I wouldn't mind a weekend on the boat."

Mary softened. "I'm proud of you, you know."

Sean exhaled. "I couldn't have done it without you. Thanks for letting me do this."

"See you soon."

He hung up, took one last look at the plant behind him, then got in his jeep and pulled out of the lot.

The work was never really done. But for the first time in a long time, he didn't need to be the one leading it—and that was the biggest win of all.

About the Author

Dr. Shane Wentz is a nationally recognized transformation leader with a proven track record of driving operational excellence and embedding Gemba-style leadership—go and see—as a cultural norm. Known for his dynamic approach and real-world results, Shane is a sought-after speaker and thought leader who has presented at conferences around the globe.

A Lean Six Sigma Master Black Belt, Shane served 20 years in the U.S. Army before holding leadership roles at Siemens, Nike, and Radial (formerly eBay Enterprises). Drawing from his military and corporate experience, he and his wife Susie co-founded *A Change in Latitude Consulting*, a boutique consulting firm that partners with organizations to deliver bottom line results through continuous improvement, project management and leadership development, training, and consulting.

Outside of his professional work, Shane is a dedicated husband of 26 years to his wife Susie, and they are proud parents to their eleven-year-old son, Tommy—and their spirited Golden Doodle, Ries.

Printed in Dunstable, United Kingdom

67792812R00097